FAITH COMETH

FAITH COMETH

CONRAD MURRELL

Adapted by MARK J. GOODSON

Study Guide by KEITH T. GOODSON

Edited by BEN ZEISLOFT

Edited by AMBER GOODSON

In honor of the Gospel legacy of Conrad Murrell.

"For I am already being poured out as a drink offering, and the time of my departure has come. I have fought the good fight, I have finished the course, I have kept the faith. In the future there is laid up for me the crown of righteousness, which the Lord, the righteous Judge, will award to me on that day, and not only to me, but also to all who have loved His appearing."

2 Timothy 4:6-8

CONTENTS

PREFACE

Many men have made a lasting impact on my life in terms of discipleship, mentorship, and Biblical training, but the influence of Brother Conrad Murrell was one of the most significant.

Growing up, my family would travel once or twice per year to a weeklong Bible camp in Bentley, Louisiana, where we would spend the week in fellowship, the singing of hymns, and doctrinally sound Biblical preaching from the pulpit multiple times throughout each day. It was a blessed time of admonishment, conviction, refreshment, and encouragement in the Lord.

Though I did not spend much time with Brother Conrad while going to these Bible camps, the impact of his preaching and the testimony of his Gospel legacy echoes in my life to this day. I am grateful for the Lord's providence in placing me in his ordained time and place to be influenced by Brother Conrad, and I pray that his Gospel legacy will shine forth through this book.

Faith Cometh is a significant book for our time, addressing the rampant emphasis on human sovereignty in matters of faith, regeneration, conversion, and salvation. Man has taken it upon himself to be the means by which he believes he is saved, and in many cases, the end by which he remains saved. He suppresses the truth concerning the absolute sovereignty of God over all and His work through Christ who lived the perfect life we could never live, died the death that we deserved for our sins, and rose to life so that we can walk in newness of life. Salvation is all of God and none of man. He did all the work and we have no reason to boast. This is the Good News.

In *Faith Cometh*, Brother Conrad patiently walks the reader through what faith is, how one attains faith, how one puts faith into practice, and how faith is strengthened in the life of the believer. This book is a must-read for your growth in the understanding and knowledge of the free gift of faith. I hope this book blesses you.

Originally, *Faith Cometh* was published in 1976 under Brother Conrad Murrell's Saber Publications, eventually renamed GATE (Grace and Truth Enterprises) Publications. I am deeply grateful to Brothers Mack Tomlinson, Mark LaCour, Gary Gatch, and Ken Murrell for granting permission to republish this important work for a new generation. Brother Conrad was never a fan of others altering an author's or preacher's message to water down its original intent. Our aim is to keep his message unchanged and uncompromised, preserving its original meaning. With that in mind, and with the permission of these faithful men of God, who knew him more closely than I did, my wife Amber and I have committed to republishing as many of Brother Conrad's books and GATE Post articles as possible. We are already working on several books, carefully revising and adapting them for readability and clarity, while ensuring with great meticulous effort that Brother Conrad's original intent is preserved.

While Brother Conrad's original works pulled Scripture references from the King James Bible, we have chosen to pull all Scripture references from the Legacy Standard Bible. Likewise, we have updated sentence structures, grammar, punctuation, and spelling to provide a more precise delivery of Brother Conrad's writings while working hard with extreme care to keep his original intent intact.

Without the editing efforts of Ben Zeisloft, the amount of careful editing and proofreading to increase the readability and clarity of this great work would be impossible. We look forward to working together again on the rest of Brother Conrad's works. This is only the beginning.

In addition, we have teamed up with my brother, Keith T. Goodson, to provide insights from Christendom, scriptures to ponder, and questions for reflection, and we have provided book recommendations at the end of each chapter and in the appendixes at the end of the book. Thank you, Keith!

We pray that this book edifies, challenges, encourages, and convicts you, the reader, for the glory of God and the good of Christendom. We hope it is helpful in the spiritual growth of a multitude of believers for many generations to come, and we thank you for your support.

— Mark J. Goodson, Grace and Truth Press L.L.C.

CONCERNING QUESTIONS FOR REFLECTION

"He who believes in Him is not judged; he who does not believe has been judged already, because he has not believed in the name of the only begotten Son of God" (John 3:18).

I believe that Brother Conrad Murrell has written a very useful, Biblically-based book on faith. It is the goal of this work to provide a series of reflections by which one might capture some of the main points of the book and compare them to the Scriptures. May both the book and the accompanying reflections aid and bless those who use them, in Jesus' name, for the glory of God and the Good of Christendom. Amen!

— Keith T. Goodson

"The way of salvation is stated in Scripture in the very plainest terms, and yet, perhaps, there is no truth about which more errors

have been uttered, than concerning the **faith** which saves the soul. Well has it been proved by experience, that all doctrines of Christ are mysteries—mysteries, not so much in themselves, but because they are hid to them that are lost, in whom the God of this world hath blinded their eyes. So plain is Scripture, that one would have said, 'He that runs may read;' but so dim is man's eye, and so marred is his understanding, that the very simplest truth of Scripture he distorts and misrepresents. And indeed, my brethren, even those who know what **faith** is, personally and experimentally, do not always find it easy to give a good definition of it. They think they have hit the mark; and then, afterwards, they lament that they have failed. Straining themselves to describe some one part of faith, they find they have forgotten another, and in the excess of their earnestness to clear the poor sinner out of one mistake, they often lead him into a worse error. So that I think I may say that, **while faith is the simplest thing in all the world, yet it is one of the most difficult upon which to write; because from its very importance, our soul begins to tremble while speaking of it, and then we are not able to describe it so clearly as we would."**

CHARLES SPURGEON

INTRODUCTION

Faith, by which a man is justified, is the great theme of the Reformation. Faith, however, has become a word in the mouth of ignorant religionists and unethical charlatans that bears no resemblance to the true Biblical doctrine.

Many ears have become accustomed to hearing such terms as "seed faith," by which you give the preacher some money, and God, in turn, makes you rich, or "faith promise," in which you pledge to give a specific amount to a religious cause, believing that God will provide, or "turning your faith loose," or "putting God on the spot" by an act of faith. In this modern age, faith is a commodity through which to work miracles, attain riches for yourself, heal the sick, and raise money. It has become a coveted accessory to Christianity because those who can discover the secret to obtaining and using faith believe there are no limits to their potential or what they can achieve.

We therefore see a multitude of preachers and writers focusing on faith. Some of them are overzealous, woefully ignorant men. Others are, forgive me, nothing less than religious pimps. They are purveyors of religious nonsense, catering to the carnal lusts of unconverted men or childish Christians.

The racket is enormously profitable: while the audience is told about faith, caught up in the throes of irrational excitement generated by the promise of great things ahead, the charlatan is preying on their eager audience. They give you an opportunity to "try your faith" by giving everything you have to them. By the time you find out the scam does not work as promised, they are long gone with your money in their pockets.

All of this is wicked enough, but it is not the chief mischief. The worst thing about it is that it has befouled the waters around the very fountain of life. It has clouded the meaning of faith itself, which is the most important subject of the Bible.

It may be well argued that love is greater than faith and that Jesus Christ is the most important person in the Bible, but the sinner has access to neither except through faith (Rom. 5:1-5). Faith is not an accessory to Christianity; it is the very essence of Christianity. Four times the Bible declares that the just shall live by faith (Hab. 2:4; Romans 1:17; Gal. 3:11; Heb. 10:38). We are not justified by a "profession of faith," as modern evangelism asserts, but by a walk of faith. Faith in God is the whole life of the believer in Jesus Christ, not something he can take or leave. It is impossible to please God without faith (Heb. 11:6). All devotions, prayers, sacrifices, tears, penances, and services mean nothing until a man believes God, and the value of his work can be measured in exact proportion to how much faith in God is involved in that work. *This is the work of God, that you believe in Him whom He has sent"* (John 6:29).

Do you desire to know what work it is that God wants you to do? Then this is it. Believe Him. Nothing else matters until you do, and when you do, you will find yourself in a work of faith.

If the religious work in which you are engaged can function without the supernatural hand of God, then it requires no faith on your part and is worthless in the sight of God. The Christian life begins, continues, and culminates in faith. Nothing less pleases Him, and you are capable of nothing greater.

WHAT FAITH IS NOT

THE MOST STUBBORN obstacle to truth is not ignorance but lies. To the innocent and unlearned, the word falls on clean, receptive soil, unhindered by preconceived ideas. But to seasoned believers, which will describe most readers of this book, the pure seed of truth must try to find a lodging in soil that is full of thorns and weeds accumulated through false teaching about faith over the years. It is therefore necessary that the first things we discuss here must be negative. All of the false ideas of faith must be cast down, or they will constantly rear themselves up in the mind of the reader, taking exception to the revealed truth.

We must consider, one by one, those things that we Christians generally call faith and demonstrate that they are manifestly *not* faith as defined by the Bible. It will become apparent as we continue that some of these notions are directly against faith, and some are the exact opposite.

Faith is not a state of mind. Faith does involve an intellectual state. The mind is involved, but a mere opinion or conviction is not faith. As James pointed out, *"the demons also believe, and shudder"* (James 2:19). Do they have faith? Are they justified by their believing? Of course not, although their "believing" is of a higher quality than that of the converts of modern day evangelism. At least they tremble, which is an exceedingly rare phenomenon today.

Yet faith is more than a frame of mind about an object. It is something you *do* that can be seen. Otherwise, why did James ask that he might see it? (James 2:18).

Not only does a state of mind fail to constitute faith, but sometimes faith is exercised when knowledge or intelligence contributes seemingly little. When King Nebuchadnezzar made a golden image and commanded everyone to fall down and worship it at the sound of prescribed music, Shadrach, Meshach, and Abednego refused to comply. The king then promised to throw them into a burning furnace: *"What god is there who can save you out of my hands?"* (Dan. 3:15). The king challenged the faith of the three men. Notice they were not able to say that they were of the opinion that God would deliver them, but that God was able. *"But if not, let it be known to you, O king, that we are not going to serve your gods, and we will not worship the golden image that you have set up"* (Dan. 3:18).

That is a confession of faith. It is made in view of the second commandment. *"You shall not make for yourself an idol —any likeness of what is in heaven above or on the earth beneath or in the water under the earth. You shall not worship them or serve them"* (Deut. 5:8-9). Their act of obedience was in view of what God *had said,* although they could not say what He *would do.* You do not have to know the outcome to act in faith. This draws to mind the second false idea of faith.

Faith is not assurance. These are two different words with completely different meanings. Many people have false assurance yet no faith. Have you ever felt perfect assurance that something was going to turn out a certain way, and then see it turn out exactly opposite? Have you ever been sure about something and then discovered you were wrong? Even so, I fear many people have an assurance of salvation who have no faith and will surely be surprised to wake up in hell.

This comes, to a great degree, from false teaching about faith and from reversing the order of faith and assurance. Many precious saints live a life of faith and never have any abiding assurance. I do not think this is desirable or necessary, but nevertheless, this life is far safer than being deceived under a false assurance in which there has never been real Biblical faith. John Bunyan, a mighty saint of God, whose classic writings have blessed millions, never had a consistent assurance, yet his life demonstrates a paragon of Biblical faith, and his fruits are those of a man of God.

Assurance comes through continued faith and a progressive revelation of the goodness of God and His design in grace toward us. We gain hope through faith and, continuing in faith, are assured (Heb. 6:11; 2 Pet. 1:5-10). You need not consider yourself faithless if you lack assurance and are yet obedient. If, however, you have assurance in disobedience, you have good reason to believe that assurance is false.

Let me give one illustration. God had determined to set His people free from their Egyptian bondage. He had demonstrated His power in a number of miracles and plagues upon Egypt, but Pharoah stubbornly refused to release them. God promised one more plague He would bring upon Pharoah and upon Egypt, and the children of Israel would surely be set free. He would pass through the land of Egypt and smite the firstborn in every house so that they die. The Israelites were to kill a lamb and apply the blood upon the sideposts and the upper doorpost of their homes wherein they lived and then were to eat the lamb. God promised to spare the house on which blood was applied.

Let us consider two possible attitudes of Jewish householders to these tidings. Here is one man who, upon hearing the command of God and the threat of the death of his first-born, does not take the threat too seriously. He is quite busy all day making final preparations to leave Egypt and does not get around to killing the lamb and applying the blood, but he has assurance about the matter. "God is a good God. He will not kill our little boy. He knows I have been busy all day and just have not had time to do what He told us we should. Everything is going to be alright. There is nothing to worry or be concerned about."

Here is the second man. The prospect of all the firstborns in Egypt dying strikes fear into his heart. He is alarmed and diligently obeys all that God has said to do. Even after slaying the lamb and applying the blood, he has no assurance about the safety of his child. All night long he is uneasy, constantly checking to see if his son is safe. When God came through Egypt that night, what was He looking for? He was not looking to see if the people were frightened or comfortable. He was looking for blood. And when He saw the blood, He saw faith.

Faith is not a frame of mind, a conviction, or assurance. Faith is something you do, in view of who God is and what He has said. It must be readily consented that faith does involve a state of mind and a strong conviction of an object, but that in itself does not constitute faith. Such a degree of conviction is necessary to commit one to the object of his faith and act upon it, but this may or may not produce comfortable assurance in it.

Men also manifestly are convincingly deceived at times. This certainly could not be called Biblical faith. A more specific word is given about this aspect of faith in chapter five when Hebrews 11:1 is considered. The walk of faith is the walk and behavior of a people whose hearts are set on obedience to God. They do not *necessarily* have assurance about the outcome of their obedience, but they are sure that they cannot bear the consequences of disobedience.

Faith is faithfulness. A faithful people are a people whose hearts are set on following the Lord. Assurance is desirable and blessed, but it is the reward, not the substance, of faith.

Promotion is not faith. While preaching a series of meetings at a church in Georgia a few years ago, another pastor came by the pastor's home where I was staying. He was bubbling over with excitement about how he was learning all about faith. He had already "believed God" for several things and received them, and he was then believing God for a riding lawn mower. "It won't be long before I will have it," he declared. "I have already announced it in church twice, describing exactly the kind God is going to give me."

That is not faith. That is promotion! Sooner or later someone is going to "feel led" to buy him a riding lawn mower to get God off the hook. After all, he has believed God for it, and if he does not now receive it, he will become disillusioned about God. Someone will have to do something to save God's face and the preacher's faith.

Preachers of this sort of faith will defend their position by saying that people must declare their faith, meaning they must tell exactly what they are believing God for. Then they will cite supposed Biblical examples of such behavior.

There are many, but one example is found in the words of Abraham to the young men and his son, Isaac: *"Stay here with the donkey while I and the boy go over there; and we will worship, and we will return to you"* (Gen. 22:5), as well as *"God will provide for Himself the lamb for the burnt offering, my son"* (Gen. 22:8). Another example is found in the words of Elisha the prophet to Naaman, the commander of the army of the king of Aram: *"Go and wash in the Jordan seven times, and your flesh will be restored to you and you will be clean."* (2 Kings 5:10).

We have no argument with the prophetic declarations

that come as a direct revelation of God's purpose. But note this carefully. In every instance, the reality declared is totally beyond the ability of the hearer's human means to perform. They had to be supernatural works of God. None hearing the prophecy could fulfill it. It had to be God.

Were these declarations made to prove that the person had faith? Most certainly not. The prophets would have shuddered at the thought. They were made to prove *God* was faithful. Often, simple Christians, in their anxiety and strong desire to prove they have faith, declare something that they have not seen with spiritual vision. Then they have to stretch and strain circumstances to make it appear that what they said was a declaration of faith. This sort of bondage is saddled upon Christians through an erroneous teaching about faith.

I visited a city in Louisiana a few years ago for a series of meetings. During that visit, a pastor greeted me with a big smile and a confident declaration that we would have revival. "We are believing God for revival this week," he declared. During the announcement time he not only talked about the revival we were going to have but the "200 we are going to have in Sunday school next Sunday." Then he asked everyone who was believing God for revival that week and 200 in Sunday school next Sunday to raise their hands.

When it came time for me to speak, I simply observed that one of two things was true. The first possibility is that we would see revival that week and 200 in Sunday School the next Sunday, or the second possibility would surely be true, namely that everyone present, including the preacher, had lied. If they were truly believing God with Biblical faith and assurance, then what they were believing would happen. Otherwise, they were not believing and were simply lying when they said they were believing. I do not doubt they were trying to believe, but that has no more substance than down-right unbelief.

Carnal desire is not faith. Faith is often preached as a tool to obtain blessings from God. It is a gimmick which, when used correctly, can produce an abundance of worldly possessions. The argument goes that God has placed all of the good things on this earth for His people. Does He not intend for us to have the best of everything? Why should God's people let the devil's crowd get all the goodies? One prominent evangelist even went so far as to recently state that if you are a Christian living in poverty, it is an indication that you are not right with God.

The apostle Paul has some strong words about such men when he calls them *"conceited, understanding nothing but having a morbid interest in controversial questions and disputes about words, out of which arise envy, strife, slander, evil suspicions, and constant friction between men of depraved mind and deprived of the truth, who suppose that godliness is a means of gain"* (1 Tim. 6:3-5). When we consider that the apostle Paul was addressing *"slaves"* (1 Tim. 6:1) at that time, it becomes clearer that he was dealing with such a perversion of truth as we are now. It seems that some of these proud and ignorant men were misleading these slaves into believing that their impoverished circumstances were proof of their lack of true faith in God.

Such unwholesome teachings come from envious, covetous, worldly men. Do they not know that Satan is declared to be the prince of this world and that it was he, not God, who offered it all to the Savior, asserting that it was within his power to give the world to anyone he wished? Jesus did not dispute the devil's claim. He only declared His intention to serve the Lord God without the enticement of carnal motivation.

Recently I met with a man whose pastor I had been a

number of years ago. In the course of inquiring about his family, I asked him about his son. "He's a Buddhist," he said. "A Buddhist!" I exclaimed. "How did that happen?" This is the story he told me. While in Japan, he met and became involved with a Japanese girl and ultimately married her. She became pregnant and gave birth to twin boys who, having birth defects, lived a short while and died. He was out of work and in impoverished circumstances. All this time, he had been trying to resolve the religious conflict with his wife by trying to move her to become a Christian. Finally, she made him a proposition. "Pray to Buddha for thirty days," she told him, "and if Buddha does not deliver us in that time, then I will become a Christian." He did as she proposed. On the twenty-ninth day, he received a call from a large firm with a fabulous job offer. He became a Buddhist.

His father asked him, "Why do you want to serve that false god?" He replied, "Why should I serve Jesus? He never gave me anything but poverty, two deformed babies that died, and a hard time. Buddha has given me a good job, lots of money, and two fine healthy children. I travel all over the world and live as I please. Why shouldn't I serve Buddha?"

Now someone may immediately object that this illustration does not apply since the boy was praying to Buddha. What difference does it make what you name your god if you have nothing but an idol in your heart? There were false "Jesuses" in the days of Paul, and there are still plenty of false Christs: demon spirits who are the dynamic behind every form of idolatry, and who will answer the prayers of the idolator. Such is the snare one falls into when he attempts to serve God for mammon. He will serve a god, but not the Savior of the Bible. An image may be only the imagination of the mind and the heart, but it is an image nonetheless.

Such a person does not have his heart set upon God, but upon the things he wants from God. Be careful that you are not guilty of the very behavior of which Satan accused Job. *"Does Job fear God without cause? Have You not made a hedge about him and his house and all that he has, on every side? You have blessed the work of his hands, and his possessions have increased in the land"* (Job 1:9-10). Satan was wrong in the case of Job. Is he wrong in your case? Are you delighted with God, or in what you receive from God?

Carnal ambition is not faith. This is simply another variety of the idolatry described above. An example is given when God speaks to Ezekiel concerning the elders of Israel:

"Then some elders of Israel came to me and sat down before me. And the word of Yahweh came to me, saying, 'Son of man, these men have set up their idols in their hearts and have put right before their faces the stumbling block of their iniquity. Should I be inquired by them at all? Therefore speak to them and tell them, thus says Lord Yahweh, any man of the house of Israel who sets up his idols in his heart, puts right before his face the stumbling block of his iniquity, and then comes to the prophet, I Yahweh will be brought to give him an answer in light of it, in light of the multitude of his idols, in order to seize the house of Israel by their heart, those who are estranged from Me through all their idols.'" (Ezekiel 14:1-5).

In the Old Testament, when men sought the Lord, they often would "inquire of the Lord" through one of His prophets. Today, of course, men of evangelical Christianity pray directly by means of the access given to us in Christ Jesus.

Ezekiel the prophet was facing men who were "inquiring of the Lord." God said, however, that they had idols in their hearts. The imaginations of men's minds are nothing but "images" upon which their hearts fondly dwell. While outwardly they say they are seeking the Lord, the image of what they really seek is in their minds and hearts.

A person conceives an objective in his mind. He sets his heart on attaining that objective. He, in his imagination, can see himself as having obtained it, and that image in his mind becomes an idol he worships and will do anything to achieve. In the business world, this may be a financial success. In the political world, this may be political power. But in the religious world, it is usually a religious success. A preacher sets a goal to pastor a church of a certain size. An evangelist sets a goal for a specific number of converts. A writer sets out to make a name for himself in the publishing world. A Christian sets his heart on obtaining a certain spiritual gift.

Although all of this is undertaken with repeated pious utterances such as, "for the glory of God," or "for souls," or "for the good of the church," the real driving power behind these visions is the image in the mind of having attained the desired success. Success thus replaces God as the central figure in the heart of man. Satan now has an idol behind which he can work.

God says, *"I Yahweh will be brought to give him an answer in light of it, in light of the multitude of his idols"* (Ezek. 14:4). The Lord will let a man have his idols. He will let him obtain his goals, his successes, and his so-called gifts, and yet leave him in his deception. *"I, Yahweh, will be brought to answer him in My own person"* (Ezek. 14:7). *"I will set My face against that man and make him a sign and a proverb, and I will cut him off from among My people"* (Ezek. 14:8).

"Delight yourself in Yahweh; And He will give you the desires of your heart" (Ps. 37:4). This is a precious promise, but modern preachers have misused this promise. Those who delight in faithfully obeying the Lord find Him graciously supplying their needs and desires, yet their faith is not turned in the direction of their desires but toward the Lord.

Prosperity and success are indicative of nothing. They certainly do not testify of faith.

Presumption is not faith. A pediatrician practicing in Tennessee near a large fundamental Christian college complained about being taken advantage of by several students from the college. They would bring their children for treatment and then explain that they were unable to pay for her services since they were "living by faith." As the doctor was a Christian and wanted to do what was right, she was confused as to the legitimacy of this excuse.

Let us examine what these students were saying. "We are believing God, but God is not meeting our needs. We are faithful, but God is not. We are believing Him, but He is not giving us enough money to pay our bills. We are doing our part, but God is not." Is this not what they were saying?

Are they not slandering God and blaspheming the Gospel with such poppycock? That is not faith. That is presumption and closer to unbelief. If they were, as they said, living by faith, then they would possess the needed money, for God is faithful. He does not call you out on a limb, saw the limb off, and expect some man to catch you when you fall.

I have puzzled many people after a "step of faith" did not work out. "But God confirmed it," they say when I question if that "step of faith" may have been presumption instead of faith. I then ask, "How did God confirm it?" The answer is often "I put out a fleece," or "He told the wife the same thing," or "the door was opened."

None of these are infallible confirmations. The devil can pour buckets of water in your fleeces or wring them out as fast as they become wet with dew. The real confirmation comes when the Midianites run from you. Do not be afraid to say, "I made a mistake." It is a fool indeed who refuses to admit that he may have been deceived and missed the will of

God. To maintain such a position is to slander God, to blaspheme the truth, and to abide in continual defeat.

If you have made a mistake, admit that mistake, go back to where you got off track, pick up where you left off, and continue onward. God is pleased with faith, not presumption.

Insights from Christendom

"Our faith in Christ wavers not so much when real arguments come against it as when it looks improbable... when the whole world takes on that desolate look which really tells us more about the state of our passions than about reality... When we exhort people to Faith as a virtue, to the settled intention of continuing to believe certain things, we are not exhorting them to fight against reason. The intention of continuing to believe is required because, though Reason is divine, human reasoners are not. When once passion takes part in the game, the human reason, unassisted by Grace, has about as much chance of retaining its hold on truths already gained as a snowflake has of retaining its consistency in the mouth of a blast furnace. Reason may win truths: without Faith she will retain them just so long as Satan pleases. There is nothing we cannot be made to believe or disbelieve. If we wish to be rational, not now and then, but constantly, we must pray for the gift of Faith, for the power to go on believing not in the teeth of reason, but in the teeth of lust and terror and jealousy and boredom and indifference that which reason, authority, or experience, or all three, have once delivered to us for truth."

C.S. LEWIS

Meditating On The Word

Read and reflect on James 2:14-26.

Questions for Reflection

1. In your own words, how would you define faith?
2. According to the author in this chapter, what is faith?
3. List six things that faith is not.
4. What has God revealed to you about faith through this chapter?

For Further Reading

Read *Faith: What It Is and What It Leads To* by Charles Spurgeon.

FIRST MENTION BASICS OF FAITH

THERE IS A PRINCIPLE OF HERMENEUTICS, which is the science of Scripture interpretation, that states the first time a subject is mentioned in the Bible, all of its foundational principles are present. How valid this is in all cases we are not prepared to argue, but it seems to hold well in the subject of faith.

We find it first mentioned in Deuteronomy 32:9-20:

"For Yahweh's portion is His people; Jacob is the allotment of His inheritance. He found him in a desert land, and in the howling waste of a wilderness; He encircled him; He cared for him; He guarded him as the pupil of His eye. Like an eagle that stirs up its nest, that hovers over its young, He spread His wings and caught them; He carried them on His pinions. Yahweh alone guided him, and there was no foreign god with him. He made him ride on the high places of the earth, and he ate the produce of the field; And He made him suck honey from the rock, and oil from the flinty rock, curds of cows, and milk of the flock, with fat of lambs, and rams, the breed of Bashan, and goats, with the finest of the wheat—and of the blood of grapes you drank wine.

But Jeshurun grew fat and kicked—you grew fat, thick, and sleek— then he abandoned God who made him, and treated the Rock of his salvation with wicked foolishness. They made Him jealous with strange gods; With abominations they provoked Him to anger. They sacrificed to demons who were not God, to gods whom they have not known, new gods who came lately, whom your fathers did not dread. You neglected the Rock who begot you, and forgot the God who brought you forth.

And Yahweh saw this and spurned them because of the provocation of His sons and daughters. Then He said, 'I will hide My face from them; I will see what their end shall be; For they are a perverse generation, Sons in whom is no faithfulness."

It is significant that the first mention of faith is in the negative sense. *No faithfulness.* No faith. That is exactly where God finds us: utterly faithless. It is in a state of wicked unbelief under which all mankind lay when Jesus came to die for us. We cannot understand the true nature of faith and grace until we see the exceeding wickedness of unbelief.

There are some who say that since Christ died for all of our sins, then men cannot go to hell for their sins but for their unbelief. The fallacy behind this is obvious since this claim does not consider unbelief to be a sin. Yet unbelief is the most heinous of all sins and is at the root of every other sin. It is indeed the cause of the damnation of men, but primarily because it is the sin of all sins against God.

Why Unbelief Is So Wicked

The reasonableness of faith. We can categorize beliefs into three groups: beliefs that are effortlessly accepted, beliefs that are moderately easy to accept, and beliefs that are difficult to accept. The categorization is not determined by the presence or absence of supporting evidence, but by our inclinations: some beliefs we desire to accept, some beliefs hold no consequence whether they are true or not, and some beliefs would rather reject.

Let me elaborate with an example: Suppose someone approaches me and compliments me, saying I am handsome with a pleasing personality. While I may lack substantial evidence to support this view and may even have evidence against this view, it would be quite easy for me to believe this claim simply because I want it to be true.

Suppose a mother has a wayward son. He lies, steals, cheats, and displays laziness and selfishness. Despite being caught and reprimanded numerous times, he repeatedly promises to change his ways. The mother is well aware of his fundamentally flawed behavior, yet she desperately wishes to believe he is good. Every little bit of evidence that shows improvement becomes an excuse for her to readily believe that he is changing for the better. Others, knowing the true nature of the boy, find his supposed change dubious. However, the desire of the mother to believe is so strong that her belief overshadows the compelling evidence against it, instead wrongly focusing on meager evidence.

This example illustrates how our natural inclination to believe something we wish to be true can lead us to downplay strong evidence to the contrary and exaggerate minimal supporting evidence. In matters of Biblical truth, people may grasp onto even the most absurd doctrines without Biblical backing, solely because they wish to believe in them.

Let us now consider beliefs that are relatively easy to believe, which will not significantly impact how I live whether they are true or not.

In my early years of school, I was taught that Columbus discovered America in 1492, and I believed this claim. I similarly learned that George Washington was our first president, and I accepted that without any trouble. I do not recall being provided with supporting evidence for these historical facts, but it was effortless for me to trust the accounts of historians. The reason is clear: whether these facts are true or not, they will not affect my personal life or my actions. They do not interfere with the plans I have for my own life.

I was also taught that the sun was 93 million miles away from the Earth and much larger than the Earth. If placed side by side, the Earth would look like a pea beside a basketball. I never had any trouble believing that claim. I have not been to space with a measuring device trying to validate that information. I just believed. I did not need supporting evidence. The words of the scientist are enough for me. Those facts do not interfere with my life. As long as the sun shines on me in the daytime, warms my body, helps my food grow, and disappears at night so I can sleep, I do not particularly care how big it is or how far away it is.

Now, since we do not have any difficulty accepting those facts as true without supporting evidence, why do we have so much difficulty believing God? Why do men subscribe to the unsupported and confusing theories of evolution rather than the simple, straightforward Biblical account of creation? Why will they insist on theories of the innate goodness of man rather than the Biblical declaration of his moral ruin and utter depravity?

All around them, they see the plain evidence of the inherent wickedness in man. They cannot even deny the wickedness in themselves. The Biblical faith is the only reasonable truth to believe. Yet men prefer to deny the truth and believe the humanistic lie.

Why, in the face of all reason, will men refuse to believe that God has appointed a day for settling accounts, where He, the just Judge of all the earth, will judge every man according to his deeds? Why, among those who confess there is a God and a way of salvation, do they refuse to believe that only He can save and that He saves on His own terms according to His own purpose? Reason dictates that God cannot be less than sovereign in all things, since otherwise He is not God. If anyone can thwart His hand from His intended purpose, then that person who stays the hand of God is himself God instead.

The reason is clearly stated by the apostle Paul: *"In order that they all may be judged who did not believe the truth, but took pleasure in unrighteousness"* (2 Thess. 2:12). The truth of God's Word interferes with my personal plans and the unrighteous pleasures I enjoy.

Evolution leaves no room for God in the universe, making me my own god: I can do as I please. My ego tells me that I am a pretty nice fellow. "Everyone ought to love me because I am basically good. I do not want to accept anything else. I want to believe that I can cheat and lie, use everyone I can to my own advantage, and get away with my infractions. If there is a God and people need salvation, I want to be saved when and how I please, according to my own terms. This is why, as a natural man, I cannot believe the truth of God's Word."

Many people superficially accept certain truths of the Bible. Take the resurrection, which is a beautiful notion, especially in the springtime when birds are singing and flowers are blooming, life springing forth from the death of winter. Nature renewing itself mirrors the concept of life emerging from death. But what does the resurrection of Christ in its true perspective mean to a sinner? It means since He indeed rose from the dead, then He was crucified as the Bible said.

He was buried a mangled and bloody mass of flesh and bones after having suffered an indescribably horrible death. This horrible death signifies the wrath of God against me in my sins. It means that *I* have, by my own wicked hands, crucified the Son of God. It also means that the same Jesus whom I played a role in crucifying is now my sovereign Lord, and I am at His mercy (Acts 2:23-36).

This old, natural man cringes at these facts. He would rather find an excuse to not believe them. Despite abundant evidence supporting their truth, he still cannot accept them. He does not want to accept them. He prefers to take pleasure in his unrighteous ways. Consequently, he rejects the well-established truth and embraces an unsupported lie (Rom. 1:18-32).

Unbelief has been nourished in grace. "Do you think lightly of the riches of His kindness and forbearance and patience, not knowing that the kindness of God leads you to repentance?" (Rom. 2:4). Our text in Deuteronomy demonstrates that Jacob had every reason to believe in God. He found Jacob when he was lost and unable to save himself. God led him when he had no sense of his own way. He *taught* Jacob when he was ignorant. He *kept* Jacob as the very apple of His eye. He fed and nourished him, making him strong and great. He protected him from his enemies so that none could harm him.

Is it not true for you too, my friend? Does not God make the rain fall upon the just and the unjust alike? Are not all men recipients of His benevolent goodness? Is there not plenty of evidence that Someone is looking after you? Are you so foolish as to think that your own hand has earned the abundance around you? You breathe grace, eat grace, wear grace, walk on grace, and sleep on and under and in grace. The grace of God surrounds you on every side. How can you be so wicked as to rob God of His honor and ascribe all this to yourself, luck, chance, or other men? Only one reason: you do not wish to serve Him. You want to serve yourself, so you believe the lie.

Unbelief serves other gods. Though man may imagine

himself to be taking the throne, he cannot stay there. Like foolish Adam in the garden, listening to the devil's lie that he *"will be like God"* (Gen. 3:5), he takes the bait and falls captive to Satan. The minute that man rebelled against God, he fell under the power of a lesser god. He became an idolater, and demons are the driving force behind all idolatry. *"They made Him jealous with strange gods; With abominations they provoked Him to anger. They sacrificed to demons who were not God, to gods whom they have not known, new gods who came lately, whom your fathers did not dread"* (Deut. 32:16-17).

Of course, most men will deny that they are idolaters or worshipers of the devil, but they are nonetheless. By refusing to put their confidence in God, they will surely put their confidence in some lesser object, which will likely be the object they believe is most responsible for their blessings or protection. *"Therefore they offer a sacrifice to their net and burn incense to their fishing net because through these things their portion is rich and their food is fat"* (Hab. 1:16).

The potential idols are many: insurance, job, lodging, friends, crops, land, money, political power, church, denomination, or good works. An idol can be whatever you depend upon more than God and may be no less devil worship than that practiced by a heathen with idols. The root of idolatry is in any case unbelief.

Unbelief forgets and despises God. "You neglected the Rock who begot you, and forgot the God who brought you forth" (Deut. 32:18). Having found other sources that seem to supply his needs and enrich him, man completely forgets Who lifted him out of the mire. The other gods allow him to live more as he pleases, think as he pleases, and congratulate himself on his own achievements. What need does he now have for God? He puts God out of his mind and constantly dwells on his idols. No man can serve two masters. He will love one and despise the other.

You cannot be neutral toward God. He must be to you either God or nothing. Without faith, it is impossible to please Him. Those who come to Him must believe that He is and that He is a rewarder of those who diligently seek Him. You cannot believe the first "He is" without the second. If God is, then He is the God that rewards those who diligently seek Him. You cannot, therefore, truly believe that He is without diligently seeking Him in faith, believing that He is your rewarder. Those who do not seek Him in this way despise Him. They seek another god whom they suppose will reward them.

The Design of Grace

"For this reason it is by faith, in order that it may be according to grace, so that the promise will be guaranteed to all the seed, not only to those who are of the Law, but also to those who are of the faith of Abraham, who is the father of us all" (Romans 4:16).

In the early years after my conversion, when I was taught how to evangelize and win souls, I had considerable trouble trying to find the proper place of faith in the design of grace.

I understood grace to be pure unmerited favor, that salvation was a gift of God and was freely bestowed upon us for no cause within ourselves, and that none could boast in having received salvation (Eph. 2:8-9). The entire reality depends *"on God who has mercy"* (Rom. 9:16). The trouble, however, can be illustrated in a device I had observed some evangelists use. After having preached his sermon, the preacher starts to offer an invitation to accept Christ as Savior. In order to demonstrate the offer of salvation that can be accepted or rejected at the will of the sinner, he takes a dollar bill out of his pocket and offers it to any boy or girl who will come to the front and accept it. After some time of assuring them that it is no trick and the offer is real, some little boy gingerly steps out, walks down the aisle, and receives the bill. As soon as he has the bill in his hand, he turns around and walks back to his seat with a proud and victorious smirk on his face to the envy of all the other children.

Why did they not accept it? "They did not have enough faith." Why did he? "He had faith." He is proud of the fact that he excelled above everyone else. Such a demonstration of salvation pictures to me saints in heaven strutting around and bragging about their faith which got them there. Surely they are much better than those sinners in hell who refused to trust in Christ.

The same lie is presented to us in the form of those who claim to heal by faith, to *get* spiritual gifts by faith, and to have worldly goods which they claim to have *gotten* by faith.

If this is true, then faith has no place in the design of grace but belongs properly in the realm of meritorious works. But that cannot be so. God designed salvation so that the very receiving of the gift would also come of grace.

Faith therefore is a duty wholly without merit within itself. One can never boast in his faith. To have faith is the least any man is obliged to do, and anything less is manifest wickedness in unbelief.

A mother bears a child in her womb for nine months. She suffers the travail of giving birth to him. She nurses him, feeds him, changes him, and washes him. She binds up all of his bruises and comforts him in all of his sorrows as he grows. She cares for him night and day through all his childhood diseases, sitting up late at night and rising early in the morning to care for his needs. After he is grown, should she reward him for calling her his mother? Of course not! Anything less would be unforgivable.

Having received so much from her hand, what should possess him to refuse to honor her except his own ungrateful, proud, and wicked heart? He will not allow himself to be in anyone's debt. He has his own designs and his mother does not fit into them and he would rather forget about her.

What father would not be offended when the son he has begotten forsakes him, his wisdom and goodness, and prefers to seek help from his enemy? You see now the great offense of unbelief. No wonder unbelief sends men to hell. *"He who believes in the Son has eternal life; but he who does not obey the Son will not see life, but the wrath of God abides on him"* (John 3:36).

Salvation is of faith, that it might be by grace. Faith, true Biblical faith, finds a way to bestow the gift and to still remain pure grace. It excludes any boasting of the receiver's attainment. When you hear someone telling you how to believe in God and receive blessings, bragging about how he received those blessings and how he lives by faith, you can be sure he knows neither faith nor grace. *"In this way, you also, when you do all the things which are commanded of you, say, 'We are unworthy slaves; we have done only that which we ought to have done'"* (Luke 17:10).

Enemies and Allies of Faith

Faith is a gift of God that cannot be produced or initiated by man. Faith comes from God. No one can "get" faith or instruct anyone on how to get it. Yet some things militate against faith and some things create a hospitable seedbed for faith. We will list these enemies and their converse allies.

Enemy: Self-Sufficiency. Man prefers to depend upon that which is tangible, that which is readily available at his own will, and that which he can control. If he has a choice of trusting his own ability or that of God, and he has reason to believe *he* is able, then he will not trust God. If he thinks that he can get along without God, he surely will try.

Jeshurun kicked when he waxed fat (Deut. 32:15). That is what man will always do. If he thinks he *can*, he will surely say that he *will*. The stubborn self-will of man is at the root of his sin and unbelief.

The essence of sin is found in Satan's declaration of his independence when he rebelled against God (Isa. 14:12-19). *"But you said in your heart, 'I **will** ascend to heaven; I **will** raise my throne above the stars of God, and I **will** sit on the mount of assembly in the recesses of the north. I **will** ascend above the heights of the clouds; I **will** make myself like the Most High.'"* The confident self-will of man is not an element of faith. It is a direct enemy of faith.

Self-confidence and self-will are principles of success among carnal men. They are the raw material from which an aggressive businessman builds his business and exploits smaller people. Salesmen are taught to build their ego and self-confidence in this way. But this attitude is directly contrary to the ways of God and the lifestyle of the faithful righteous. *"For we are the circumcision, who worship in the Spirit of God and boast in Christ Jesus and put no confidence in the flesh"* (Phil. 3:3).

Ally: Insufficiency, Need, Helplessness. *"How hard it will be for those who are wealthy to enter the kingdom of God"* (Mark 10:23). Jesus had just lost what any outside observer would have called an excellent prospect for his movement. He had put His finger on the problem of the rich young ruler. The young man wanted eternal life along with everything else he already had. Jesus told him that he could only have eternal life *instead* of everything else. The young man left sorrowfully. He trusted in his possessions and could not bring himself to abandon them and trust in God alone. Had he been destitute, however, this would not have been the case.

Riches are not a barrier to true faith but can be a grievous stumbling block. Neither does destitution guarantee faith in Christ. Millions of beggars will be in hell. Yet a principle that aids in faith can be seen here.

Man must be at least sensibly stripped of everything upon which he can depend. God often systematically does this for us. One by one He takes away all of our props, our securities, our loves, and our hopes until nothing is left but Himself, and then He presents Himself to us as the object of our faith.

It is the nature of man to stubbornly resist this stripping process. We do not want to be humbled to the place where we must trust God. Yet this is the only time in which we will do so. Thousands of Jesus' disciples forsook Him when He began to preach to them about the cross in the sixth chapter of John. The twelve did not, by their own confession, for one reason: they had nowhere else to go. Humanly speaking, they could have left Him, but the Savior had already wrought such a stripping work in their heart and in their lives that they could only follow Him. They had seen the futility and emptiness of everything else the world had to offer. Eternal life was nowhere else to be found. It is this desperate need that brings God's people to Him in faith.

Enemy: Lusts, Strong Desire. An act of faith depends on knowledge of the will and purpose of God in a specific sense. God reveals His will and purpose to men so that they will know what to believe Him for. But when a man is obsessed with a desire of his own, he is not free to recognize the will of God in a given matter. He interprets everything in the light of his lusts and is willing to believe only that which he thinks will work events out in the way he wants them.

"You lust and do not have, so you murder. You are envious and cannot obtain, so you fight and quarrel. You do not have because you do not ask. You ask and do not receive, because you ask with wrong motives, so that you may spend it on your pleasures" (James

4:2-3). Men who have failed to obtain what they want by violence and force now turn to the "Christian" way to fulfill their lusts. They "ask" and "believe" God, yet they will receive nothing from God, because what they have is not faith, but carnal desire.

Strong desires are not an element of faith, but an enemy of faith. They cloud the thinking and obsess the mind so that a man cannot clearly hear the voice of God. The old sinful flesh in him is raising such a clamor for what he wants that the voice of God cannot be discerned. His ways cannot be seen because the image of man's desire is constantly before his face. He cannot know the mind of God and therefore cannot believe.

Ally: The Cross. There is only one place for the flesh: the cross of Jesus Christ. The flesh cannot be reformed or remedied. The flesh must die. *"Therefore, since Christ has suffered in the flesh, arm yourselves also with the same purpose—because he who has suffered in the flesh has ceased from sin—so as to no longer live the rest of the time in the flesh for the lusts of men, but for the will of God"* (1 Pet. 4:1-2). Those who would learn faith must prepare to deny themselves, to starve out their lusts, and to yield up to the cross of Christ everything of the old Adamic nature.

The spoiled child who always gets everything he wants never grows and faces reality. He never learns the beauty, wisdom, and perfection of his parent's will because he is too busy satisfying his childish lusts. But the son who has suffered privation and self-denial is forced into facing an alternative to his own way, and he learns the way of his elder is a proven and tried way. *"For if you are living according to the flesh, you must die, but if by the Spirit you are putting to death the practices of the body, you will live"* (Rom. 8:13).

Enemy: Instability, Options. *"But he must ask in faith, doubting nothing, for the one who doubts is like the surf of the sea, driven and tossed by the wind. For that man ought not to expect that he will receive anything from the Lord, being a double-minded man, unstable in all his ways"* (James 1:6-8). Those who look to the Lord have no reserve alternatives. If a man has an option or two in case the way of the Lord does not work out, he will never trust God. He does not have to, because in his mind if God does not come through, then he has recourse elsewhere.

Do not think you are kidding God by looking to Him on a trial basis. He knows your fickle heart. You are merely sampling the possibilities and leaving plenty of open doors that you can scoot through if the situation is not suiting you. As long as you are vacillating back and forth between two or more ways, you will receive nothing from God.

An alternative possibility tucked away in the recesses of your mind wars against faith and makes faith virtually impossible. *"How long will you be limping between two opinions? If Yahweh is God, follow Him; but if Baal, follow him"* (1 Kings 18:21). The people answered him not a word. They could not. They were double-minded. They had two possible courses and they were unable to commit themselves to either.

Ally: Single-mindedness, Steadfastness. Get rid of all your alternatives and set your mind on the Lord alone. Put all your eggs in one basket. You will not truly trust the Lord until that is done.

One pastor brought a troubled man to me a few years ago for counseling. When I asked him about his problem, he replied, "I want to serve the Lord but I am having a terrible time." I asked him, "What seems to be hindering you?" He said, "Everything and everybody, it seems." I insisted, "We should get down to particulars."

"I have a smoking problem. I know I should not be smoking. It is harmful to me and a blight on my testimony, but I am having a hard time giving it up. Then there is my wife.

She thinks I am a fanatic and she says if I insist on living a Christian life, she is going to leave me. She wants to have some fun, and I do not want to go back into that kind of life, but I do not want to lose my wife. Then there is my business partner. He is not a Christian and we are having a conflict over some unethical business deals he wants to pull. He says I am holding back the business with my stupid morals, and if I do not shape up, he is going to force me out. Then last week I was down in Tucson in a restaurant feeling sorry for myself and this young divorcee approached me. She liked me and made some obvious suggestions and approaches. I almost fell into what she was proposing. But I do not want to live like that. I am just in a terrible mess."

"You surely are, but maybe I can help you get some things settled," I said. "It seems to me you have about four options here. You can only take one of them, so you may as well eliminate the other three. Let's find out which ones you can take and which ones you cannot and then see what we have left. Here is your first option. You can walk out that door the same way you came in with nothing changed and nothing settled. Can you do that?"

"I don't want to," he said.

"But you can," I insisted.

"If I had not wanted help I would not have come here," he insisted back.

"But can you leave without it? Are you willing to walk out of here the same way you came in?" I repeated. "Can you do that? Can you go on living the way you are now? Think about it. Because if you can, you will. There is no use in me wrangling around here with you for two or three hours only to have you refuse to do what you must and leave the same way you came in. If you can do that, then go ahead and do it now. Let's not waste any more time."

He looked at me, saw I meant it, thought about it a bit,

and then said, "No, I cannot do that. I have got to have some help. I cannot live any longer the way I am. Something has to be settled."

"Then we can eliminate that option. It no longer exists," I continued. "Something has to be settled before you leave here tonight. Now we only have three left. Here is your second option: Forget about being a Christian and serving the Lord. Put the thought of it out of your mind and go ahead and do whatever you like. If you want to smoke, stop feeling guilty about it and puff away. If your wife wants you to go out and get drunk and raise hell with her, go ahead. If your partner wants to pull some fast deals that can make you rich and will not get you in jail, go for it. Take advantage of anybody you can, make as much money as you can, do what you like, and live it up. If you see that divorcee again, take her up on the proposition. Whatever you feel like doing, help yourself."

He stared at me incredulously.

"Can you do that?" I asked.

He shook his head, "No, I cannot do that. I cannot live that way."

I asked again, "Are you sure?"

He confirmed, "I am sure."

"Think about it now and settle it," I doubled down. "If you can do that, then you ought to go ahead because you will sooner or later. But if you cannot, then settle it in your mind that you cannot and forget about it. It is no use you ever thinking about it anymore. It is an utter impossibility."

He repeated, "I cannot do that."

Continuing, I said, "All right, that eliminates two options, and two more are left. Here is your third one: Go home and get a gun. If you do not have one at home, stop off at a pawn shop and pick yourself up a pistol. Get out in the yard so that you will not make a mess in the house for someone to clean up, take good aim so that you do not miss, and put a bullet in your brain."

He jerked his head back and stared at me. "I cannot do that. I would go to hell."

"Probably so," I said. "But at least you would not have to live in this hell till you get to the next one."

He replied, "No, I cannot do that."

I continued, "Then it looks like you have only one course left. Follow the Lord. Obey Him. If your wife leaves you, follow the Lord. If you lose your business and all your money, follow the Lord. If it costs you all your pleasures, follow the Lord. You really do not have any other option. You cannot do anything else. Live, die, swim, or sink, you must follow Him."

He thought awhile, then lifted his head, and slowly as the truth began to dawn upon him, a relieved smile spread across his worried face. "That is right, is it not? It is really very simple. He is my only hope of life. There is nothing else to do."

I prayed with him, shook his hand, and dismissed the meeting.

Nearly two years later, I was back in the same city and this man came to the meeting. His wife was with him, clinging to his arm. They had been, it seemed, through hell itself. His faith had been tried in the fire. The devil had exhausted his resources in his attempt to shake him from the commitment he made that night. But when he had left that counseling session, he was a single-minded man with only one place to go. His eyes were steadfastly fixed upon God as his deliverer. He and his wife both wore the broad sweet smiles of a victory that endures. They had learned indeed that faith is the victory that overcomes the world. Such as these can give unerring testimony that God is indeed worthy of our trust. That is faith.

Insights from Christendom

"I do not recall another period when faith was as popular as it is today. Faith has come back into favour with almost everybody. The scientist, the cab driver, the philosopher, the actress, the politician, the prize fighter, the housewife... all are ready to recommend faith as the panacea for all our ills—moral, spiritual, and economic. If we only believe hard enough we'll make it somehow. So goes the popular chant. What you believe is not important. Only believe.

What is overlooked in all this is that faith is good only when it engages truth; when it is made to rest upon falsehood it can and often does lead to eternal tragedy. For it is not enough to believe; we must believe the right thing about the right One. Let us beware that the Jesus we 'accept' is not one we have created out of the dust of our imagination and formed after our own likeness.

Faith is a gift of God to a penitent soul and has nothing whatsoever to do with the senses or the data they afford. Faith is a miracle; it is the ability God gives to trust His Son, and anything that does not result in action in accord with the will of God is not faith but something short of it.

In that great and terrible day there will be those white with shock when they find that they depended upon a mental assent to Christianity instead of upon a miracle of new birth."

A.W. TOZER

Meditating on the Word

Read and reflect on Deuteronomy 32:9-20, Romans 4:1-5, and Romans 4:23-5:2.

Questions for Reflection

1. Where does God find us?
2. In what state was humanity when Jesus came to die for us?
3. What is the most heinous of all sins?
4. Provide five reasons why unbelief is so wicked.
5. Can a person be neutral toward God? Why or why not?
6. What is a duty entirely without merit in itself?
7. Is faith a gift from God, or is it produced and initiated by man? What support can you provide for your answer from Scripture? How does this relate to the fact that faith is something you do in response to who God is and what He has said?
8. List three allies and three enemies of faith.
9. What has God revealed to you about faith in this chapter?

For Further Reading

Read *Christian Reflections* by C.S. Lewis.

3

HUMAN FAITH VERSUS SAVING FAITH

LEAFING through the current issue of a leading evangelical magazine, I came across a test for "Knowledge of Bible Doctrine." About sixteen multiple choice questions were given, one of which was, "What are the steps necessary for salvation?" Four choices were offered:

1. Repent and believe, 2. Believe and be baptized. 3. Receive Christ as Lord, and 4. Believe only.

Turning to the answer page, the editors indicated that the correct answer was the fourth choice: "Over 200 times," they explained, "the single requirement in the Bible is faith."

I sat down and wrote a letter to the editors objecting to the way they had stated and answered the question because the question strongly implied that salvation is possible without repentance. That is not true. *"I tell you, no, but unless you repent, you will all likewise perish"* (Luke 13:3-5). It also suggested that salvation is possible while rejecting Christ as Lord. That also cannot be true. To accept a Christ who is not absolute Lord is to receive another Jesus who cannot save. The Christ of the Bible saves the sinner as Lord, not as a substitute only. Our savior is our God, our Sovereign, else we have none.

Yet, the fact remains that over 200 times in the Scriptures we are told that men are justified by faith alone. *"He who believes in the Son has eternal life"* (John 3:36). *"Believe in the Lord Jesus, and you will be saved"* (Acts 16:31). *"So that He would be just and the justifier of the one who has faith in Jesus"* (Rom. 3:26). These are precious promises, and the theme of the great Reformation is built around them. We have no desire to weaken the hope in Christ men have gained through faith in the God of these precious promises.

But a problem persists. Anyone who has been engaged in evangelism for any time has certainly been met with numbers of people who believe everything the Bible says, yet have absolutely no assurance of salvation. They have no reason to believe they are in Christ Jesus. Many times "soul winners" take these passages and attempt to give such persons assurance, but this task is futile. They cannot have assurance because they are yet unconverted. How can this be so? Do they not believe? Are the promises of God not true? Can we not take God at His word?

A friend of mine who lives in a southeastern city where there is a large fundamental university related this incident to me. He was stopped on the street one morning by a man whom he knew to be unconverted.

"Pardon me, mister, are these young men with Bibles in their hands going around stopping people and talking to them, preachers?" asked the man.

My friend said, "Well, they say they are. I suppose so."

The man replied, "In that case, I have a problem."

"What is it?" my friend asked.

The man explained, "One of them stopped me this morning and read from his Bible, *'For God so loved the world, that He gave His only begotten Son, that whoever believes in Him shall not perish, but have eternal life.'* Then he asked me, 'Do you believe that?' I asked, 'Is that a Bible?' 'Yes,' he said. I replied, 'Then I believe it because I believe everything that is in the Bible.' He exclaimed, 'Bless your heart! You are saved!' 'I am?' I asked. He stated, 'Yes, you are. Now what is your name?' And with this, he took out a little book and pencil preparing to write it down. Now I did not know that this might be some sort of trick, so I gave him a fictitious name, which he wrote in the book. Then he shook my hand and told me that my name was written in the Lamb's Book of Life and that he would see me in heaven. Now my problem is this: If that is the name that is written down up there it is the wrong one. How am I going to get that straightened out?"

Such a ridiculous incident would be amusing if it were not so tragic. We have so much evangelism today that is conducted on no higher level than that account. People are told to believe, told when they have believed, and told when they are saved, yet they have no more assurance of salvation afterward than before.

Our problem is a problem of semantics. Our problem can be illustrated by this passage: *"So when He was raised from the dead, His disciples remembered that He said this; and they believed the Scripture and the word which Jesus had spoken. Now when He was in Jerusalem at the Passover, during the feast, many believed in His name, when they saw His signs which He was doing. But Jesus, on His part, was not entrusting Himself to them, for He knew all men"* (John 2:22-24). In these three verses, we have one Greek word used three times, once in each verse, and yet each time the word is used, the word has a different meaning.

Words do not have definite conclusive meanings. They have usages. This can be reasily seen in the English language. Take, for example, the word *spring*. To a farmer, it may mean the time of year that the birds begin to sing and the plants begin to grow again. To an athlete, it may mean a leap across a barrier on a track. To an engineer, it may mean a mechanical device that suspends an automobile chassis from its axles. To a geologist, it may mean an orifice or crack in the earth formation at the bottom of some hills where waters gush out of the ground. Yet it is identically the same word and has the same root meaning.

The Greek is no different. No language is so accurate that you can build a theology on grammar or a doctrine on meanings of words, nor do word study books provide a sure way of understanding what is intended by certain words. One must have a working knowledge of the whole revealed truth of God, or at least that particular truth with which he is concerned.

In the first instance in that passage from John of the Greek *pistueo*, the word is translated as *believe* and refers to *saving faith*. In the next verse, the same word is translated as *believe* and refers to *human faith*, which will save no one. In the last verse, the same word appears again and is translated as *commit* or *entrust*, and refers to the faithfulness of God. We see the same word used three times in a three-verse context, each time having a completely different meaning.

How do we know that the first verse refers to *saving faith* and the second verse refers to *human faith*? We know that the first verse speaks of *saving faith* because Jesus stated in His high priestly prayer later in John that not one of the twelve was lost except for Judas. That is the only way we know that is true. We cannot tell if the passage refers to *saving faith* with the word *believe* in the passage, but truth revealed in other parts of Scripture dictates this to be the case.

We know that the second verse speaks of *human faith* because the next verse tells us that Jesus did not *commit* or *entrust* himself unto them. We have people believing in Jesus but in whom Jesus did not believe. They were yet unconverted and as lost as they were before they met Christ. If one still has doubts that this is true, he only needs to read further down in the third chapter of John and find one of those Jews who believed in Jesus because of the miracles which he saw. He came to Jesus declaring his faith because of the miracles he witnessed. What did Jesus say to him? He said *"you must be born again"* (John 3:7). These Jews had human faith but were still unregenerate. Christ would not entrust Himself to them.

What is Human Faith?

Human Faith is a logical intellectual conclusion at which a man arrives after due consideration of reasonable evidence. This faith will save no one. This is where the damning damage is done in an evangelism that does not know the difference between human faith and saving faith.

Faith in Christ is sometimes illustrated like this: You look at a chair, take note of the materials, the structure and shape, and having drawn on previous knowledge of similar chairs in which you have sat safely, come to a logical conclusion that the chair will sustain your weight. With that conviction, you sit in the chair. Now that is good instruction for sitting in a chair, and that is human faith. But it isn't worth a dime as far as justifying faith is concerned. It has its origin and roots in man and the human reasoning process, and God is not involved.

The same idea can be projected into realities relating to God and salvation. There are plenty of good logical reasons to believe the Bible, such as the harmony of its spirit and letter, the accuracy of its prophecies, the beauty and perfection of its precepts, its massive impact on the moral character of man through the centuries, and its sheer endurance despite constant attacks. All of this comes in the face of the fact that the Bible was penned over many centuries at the hands of widely diverse men who had no opportunity to collaborate. There is overwhelming evidence that the Bible is the Word of God, even enough to stand up in any court of law in which facts are established when there can be no reasonable doubt.

The same can be said of the person of Christ. Sanity demands we believe what He said about Himself to be true. He had to be either a madman, a master deceiver, or the Son of God.

As C.S. Lewis, the converted atheist, once said, *"You can put Him in an insane asylum, lock him up in a fraud's prison, or bow down to Him as God. But no more of this patronizing nonsense about His being a good man, but nothing more than a man. That is an option He did not leave us."* A man who wanted to weigh the evidence without prejudice must believe that Jesus is God incarnate.

You cannot charge His disciples and the church fathers with perpetuating fraud. Church history, soundly supported by secular history, gives conclusive evidence of this truth. Men do not suffer shame, disgrace, privation, poverty, torture, and death for lies. The power of God transformed those men into living sacrifices and eternal testimonies of the truth of God's word. No atheist can read Foxe's *Book of Martyrs* with an unbiased mind and remain a sane unbeliever. When reason alone is confronted with all of this evidence, unbelief becomes irrational. But that resulting faith is not saving faith.

Sometimes human faith is based upon witnessing some miraculous evidence. This was the case in our text. They saw the miracles that Jesus did and therefore believed that God was on the scene. But that is not sufficient faith to convert. They were still unregenerate in heart even though they could not deny that God was working.

The signs and wonders that men are witnessing today are

not producing any converts. They are sufficient to produce human faith but nothing beyond that.

Sometimes human faith is based upon a personal experience of some kind, like an emotional catharsis, a healing, a supposed answer to prayer, an experience of the supernatural that touched one personally.

Without truth, there is no way one can know that such phenomena are a blessing from God or simply a demonic manifestation to deceive one into thinking he has a standing in grace. Such experiences are sufficient to cause one to believe in the existence of the supernatural and the reality of God, but they fall short of producing saving faith in the God of the Bible.

Why It Falls Short of Salvation

Human faith falls short of saving faith for a number of reasons. We will consider some of the more obvious ones.

Repentance is not necessary. A decision in the mind does not require repentance. It only requires intelligence. There need not be any moral change associated with this. It is not a moral act, but rather one of intelligence. It takes no account of the wickedness of men or the holiness of God, but only the existence of facts. It does not grieve over anything done in the past or make any resolve toward a particular behavior in the future. It simply believes what is so to be true.

In view of this, it ought to be obvious that such faith will not justify. There is no justification without repentance. We are not justified *by* repentance, but neither are we justified apart from it. To those who supposed that certain Galileans must have been especially wicked sinners because they were slaughtered by Pilate in the midst of their sacrifices, Jesus said, *"Do you think that these Galileans were greater sinners than all other Galileans because they suffered these things? I tell you, no, but unless you repent, you will all likewise perish"* (Luke 13:2-3).

John the Baptist, a man sent to prepare the hearts of men to believe on Christ Jesus, proclaimed repentance to the people. It is only the repentant heart that can savingly believe on Christ. When the command "only believe" is given, this command is spoken to persons already in a broken and repentant state, and whose hearts have been prepared. It is true that God does command all men to believe, and that they are justified by faith alone, but that faith is not possible in unrepentance.

The early church knew and gave record that repentance was necessary if men were to be saved. *"When they heard this, they quieted down and glorified God, saying, 'Well then, God has granted to the Gentiles also the repentance that leads to life'"* (Acts 11:18). Paul did not neglect the primacy of repentance in his instruction to Timothy. *"With gentleness correcting those who are in opposition, if perhaps God may give them repentance leading to the full knowledge of the truth, and they may come to their senses and escape from the snare of the devil, having been held captive by him to do his will"* (2 Tim. 2:25-26).

Human faith takes place without repentance and therefore produces no moral change in a person. We have multitudes of people believing in Jesus, on the way to hell, being told they are saved.

Humility and contrition are unnecessary. The essence of justification is union with Christ. It is *"Christ in you, the hope of glory"* (Col. 1:27). The indwelling life is our hope of justification and eternal life. He is the righteousness that makes us acceptable in the beloved (Eph. 1:6). *"Test yourselves to see if you are in the faith; examine yourselves! Or do you not recognize about yourselves that Jesus Christ is in you—unless indeed you fail the test?"* (2 Cor. 13:5). Paul allows only two possibilities: all who have hope have such hope because God has chosen to tabernacle Himself in them.

Isaiah describes the kind of man in whom God will tabernacle Himself and in whom He will dwell: *"For thus says the One high and lifted up who dwells forever, whose name is Holy, 'I dwell on a high and holy place, and also with the crushed and lowly of spirit in order to revive the spirit of the lowly and to revive the heart of the crushed'"* (Isa. 57:15). Christ commits Himself to the humble and broken man.

A man may intellectually believe the Bible and believe in Christ Jesus yet never be humbled or broken. In fact, multitudes exhibit rank pride in their orthodoxy. They boast in their adherence to the fundamentals of the faith. Such faith is not justifying faith because Christ is not in that faith. He resists and stands far off from a proud and haughty person.

The beatitudes recorded in the book of Matthew describe the attitudes of the blessed. They are not primarily commandments but descriptions of those who have been blessed by union with Christ Jesus. All that are blessed have these attitudes. Where these attitudes are not evident, there is no sound reason to believe the people are blessed.

Blessed are the poor in spirit; for *theirs* is the Kingdom of Heaven (Matt. 5:3). The Kingdom of Heaven belongs to the poor in spirit and only them.

Blessed are they that mourn: for *they* shall be comforted (Matt. 5:4). The mourners, those who mourn over their sins and the wickedness of the earth, shall be comforted. The Comforter, the Holy Spirit, is sent *only* to the mourners.

Blessed are the meek, for *they* shall inherit the earth (Matt. 5:5). The meek, and only the meek, shall inherit the earth.

These are descriptions of broken and contrite souls who have been humbled under the mighty hand of God. They are meek and lowly in spirit. They mourn and weep.

Just as surely as these are blessed, those who do not bear these traits are cursed. Consider the converse.

Cursed are the haughty and proud, for theirs is the prison house of darkness and damnation.

Cursed are the frivolous and foolish, they that revel and laugh in the midst of wickedness, for they shall be tormented.

Cursed are the arrogant and cocky, for they shall inherit the lake of fire.

All men are born proud. They have nothing to be proud of, but that does not stop them from strutting. If you have never been broken and humbled, then you are surely still proud.

Your human faith will not cure your pride, nor can you grasp saving faith until you become pliable clay in the hands of the Master. Only then will you begin to attain a higher faith that justifies.

Holiness is not necessary. There is no dynamic in human faith to transform man into a Christlike image. The facts are detached in such a way that they bear no compelling influence on the believer.

There are two kinds of holiness in Scripture, imputed and imparted. Imputed righteousness is legally accounted to the believer at conversion. It is perfect and is the very righteousness of the Lord Jesus Christ. Imparted righteousness comes subsequent to conversion. It is imperfect but it is being perfected as evidenced by spiritual growth. It is an actual experimental participation in the holiness of the Lord Jesus Christ. He chastens His sons so that they might be partakers of His holiness (Heb. 12:10). We are told in Hebrews that without this holiness we have no hope in Christ: *"Pursue peace with all men, and the sanctification without which no one will see the Lord"* (Heb. 12:14).

Holiness is not a prescribed list of dos and do nots that

we perform externally. Holiness is an inward attitude, a condition of the heart, and a disposition of the soul of man who has truly been born from above. We go back to the Sermon on the Mount once more.

"Blessed are they which do hunger and thirst after righteousness for they shall be filled (Matt. 5:6). All who have been genuinely converted to Christ have an unquenchable thirst for righteousness. Not only do they loathe their old life, but they long to lay hold on the full expression and experience of the New Life in Christ Jesus. The old carnal man wants to know how wicked he can be and still be saved. The new man in Christ wants to be as holy as it is possible for a man to be on earth.

Blessed are the merciful, for they shall obtain mercy (Matt. 5:7). This holy disposition is evidenced in a kind and compassionate disposition toward all men.

Blessed are the pure in heart, for they shall see God (Matt. 5:8). Only the pure in heart shall see God. The heart is turned from vile and corrupt things of this earth to the heavenly and pure things of God.

Blessed are they who are persecuted for righteousness' sake, for theirs is the Kingdom of Heaven (Matt. 5:10). The apostle assures us that all who will live godly in Christ Jesus shall suffer persecution (2 Tim. 3:12). This is a disturbing declaration in view of the ease and approval in which professing Christians live today. Is there not enough holiness about us to provoke the devil?

Although holiness is not an external action one performs, but an inward attitude he has, we must face the fact that if the real inward attitude is there, that attitude will be evidenced in an outward performance. There must be an actual separation from sin and all that is sinful. Justification is union with Christ, and Christ has no union with the devil, with darkness, with Belial, or with idols (2 Cor. 6:14-16).

"'Therefore, come out from their midst and be separate,' says the Lord. 'And do not touch what is unclean, and I will welcome you. And I will be a father to you, and you shall be sons and daughters to Me,' says the Lord Almighty" (2 Cor. 6:17-18).

Christ is not in it. There is no assurance in human faith because Christ Himself is not in it. It is Christ in you that is the hope of glory. As Calvin said, *"We are justified by faith and faith alone. But that faith is not alone: God is in it."*

This brings us to the third usage of the Greek *pistueo* in the passage from John. *"But Jesus, on His part, was not entrusting Himself to them, for He knew all men."* The word "but" indicates a departure from what might be expected. It is strongly implied that Christ *does* commit Himself to those who savingly believe in Him through true repentance.

That is a staggering thought. It is one matter for a man to commit himself to Christ, but quite another for Christ to commit Himself to a man. Yet, that is exactly the transaction that takes place in true conversion.

Although the same word is used in each case, the word is used in a different sense. I commit myself to Christ as one who entrusts an able and qualified artist with a marred portrait for restoration, a skilled mechanic with his automobile for repairs, or a trusted banker with his treasure for safekeeping. If I really trust these, I will not be constantly checking up on them to make sure they are doing the job right and are not ruining or losing what I have entrusted to him. I trust him and rest the possession in his safekeeping. Even so, I have abandoned my life at His feet, not to perform some service for Him, but for what He can do for me.

When Christ commits Himself to me, He is certainly not trusting me to take care of Him. He is pledging Himself and all that He is for my every need. He is, I say it carefully and reverently, putting Himself at my disposal, not that I am going to take charge of Him since He has already taken charge of me, but since He has accepted responsibility for me, He will spare nothing of all that He is to see that I am saved to the uttermost. All of His righteousness, His virtue, His authority and power, and His standing with the Father are mine by virtue of our union together.

Has the wonder and marvel of this great salvation struck you yet, dear reader? With what shall we compare it? Do you have a letter of commitment from your bank? To what extent have they committed themselves to you? The extent of your credit? Your collateral? Your friend's resources? All the assets of the bank?

I have a letter of commitment from God. What does that letter assure? God has committed Himself to the extent of all He is for all my needs as long as He lives! Who shall threaten or intimidate me? Let Satan roar, threaten, and intimidate those who have no hope. The eternal God is my refuge and underneath are the everlasting arms (Deut. 33:27).

Insights from Christendom

"Amazing grace! How sweet the sound!
That saved a wretch like me;
I once was lost, but now am found;
Was blind, but now I see.
'Twas grace that taught my heart to fear,
And grace my fears relieved;
How precious did that grace appear
The hour I first believed!
Through many dangers, toils, and snares,
I have already come;

'Tis grace has brought me safe thus far,
And grace will lead me home.
Yes, when this flesh and heart shall fail,
And mortal life shall cease,
I shall possess, within the vail,
A life of joy and peace.
The Lord has promised Good to me
His word my hope secures
He will my shield and portion be
As long as life endures
The earth shall soon dissolve like snow,
The sun forbear to shine:
But God, who called me here below,
Will be forever mine."

— John Newton

"And can it be that I should gain
An interest in the Savior's blood?
Died He for me, who caused His pain?
For me, who Him to death pursued?
Amazing love! How can it be
That Thou, my God, should die for me?"

— Charles Wesley

"If then sinful men find favor with God, it is 'grace upon grace!' If God vouchsafe still to pour fresh blessings upon us, yea, the greatest of all blessings, salvation; what can we say to these things, but, 'Thanks be unto God for his unspeakable gift!' And thus it is. Herein 'God commendeth his love toward us, in that, while we were yet sinners, Christ died' to save us 'By grace' then 'are ye saved through faith.' Grace is the source, faith the condition, of salvation."

JOHN WESLEY

Meditating on the Word

Read and reflect on John 2:18-24 and John 3:14-18.

Questions for Reflection

1. What is human faith?
2. Provide at least four good and logical reasons why people have human faith.
3. List four reasons why human faith falls short of saving faith.
4. In your own words, explain the difference between human faith and saving faith.
5. What has God revealed to you about faith in this chapter?

For Further Reading

Read *Man: The Dwelling Place of God* by A.W. Tozer.

FIVE LEVELS OF FAITH

THE PRECEDING chapter was given to consideration of human faith, demonstrating why such faith does not justify the sinner, and why such faith stops short of salvation. In this chapter we will view the progressive nature of saving faith.

"I am under obligation both to Greeks and to barbarians, both to the wise and to the foolish. In this way, for my part, I am eager to proclaim the gospel to you also who are in Rome. For I am not ashamed of the gospel, for it is the power of God for salvation to everyone who believes, to the Jew first and also to the Greek. For in it the righteousness of God is revealed from faith to faith; as it is written, 'But the righteous will live by faith'" (Romans 1:14-17).

A Great Salvation

The Gospel is the power of God unto salvation to the believer. It will not save the unbeliever. He does not believe it. To the unbeliever, God speaks in His holy law. It is the law that converts (Ps. 19:7), but the Gospel that saves. The law convicts and exposes the wickedness of the sinner. The law threatens with the righteous wrath of God, bringing the sinner to a realized need of the Gospel, wherein he may find salvation in Christ Jesus. But the Gospel will do nothing for any man until he becomes a believer. The Gospel is given to God's believing people.

Now I know this will be confusing to many of my readers since we are accustomed to considering a believer as already saved. This is because we have been mistaught with respect to what the Scriptures mean when they speak of salvation.

Salvation is much greater than justification. *"How will we escape if we neglect so great a salvation? That salvation, first spoken by the Lord, was confirmed to us by those who heard"* (Heb. 2:3). It is a great salvation, and is much greater than any of us know about yet, and this salvation can be neglected with the result of loss. Just what that loss might be cannot be stated in blanket terms. A man may begin with human faith, neglect that faith, and perish. The disturbing facts are before us: It is a great salvation. It can be neglected. Those who neglect it will not escape.

The Gospel is the power of God unto salvation because in it the righteousness of God is revealed from faith to faith. There is a contrast between Romans 1:17 and Romans 1:18-32. In Romans 1:17, the righteousness of God is progressively revealed from faith to faith. From Romans 1:18 through the rest of the chapter, the unrighteousness of man is progressively revealed from unbelief to unbelief. Every man is traveling in one or the other of these directions. Through believing the Gospel, he is moving from faith to faith because he is seeing more and more of the Glory of God, or through rejection of truth, he is moving from unbelief to unbelief, his foolish heart is becoming more and more darkened, and his ultimate wickedness is progressively exposed.

The positive side of progressive salvation is demonstrated

by the trilogy found in John 1:16, Romans 1:17, and 2 Corinthians 3:18.

"For of His fullness we have all received, and grace upon grace" (John 1:16). The King James Version gives an excellent translation of this verse in the words *"grace for grace."* It does not mean "one blessing and favor on top of another" as most of the modern translations render. It means that we have received grace because of grace. Only grace can cause grace. Otherwise, grace is not grace, but is reward or compensation.

"For in it the righteousness of God is revealed from faith to faith; as it is written, 'But the righteous will live by faith'" (Rom. 1:17). Faith builds upon faith. It takes faith to apprehend faith. As revelation moves, faith must also move forward or die.

"But we all, with unveiled face, beholding as in a mirror the glory of the Lord, are being transformed into the same image from glory to glory, just as from the Lord, the Spirit" (2 Cor. 3:18). As the righteousness of God is revealed and we believe, we are transformed into His likeness.

God has predestined us to be conformed to the image of His Son. That is the side revealing God's sovereignty (Rom. 8:29). *"And everyone who has this hope fixed on Him purifies himself, just as He is pure"* (1 John 3:3). That is the side of human responsibility. They both are true and stand side by side. Those of us who have received grace because of grace are moving from faith to faith through the revelation of divine righteousness in the Gospel, and are being transformed from glory to glory.

It takes faith to get faith. If you do not have any, then you cannot get any more. In the economic world, capital earns money. Money makes money, and it takes money to make more money. Jesus used this principle in one of His parables: *"For whoever has, to him more shall be given, and he will have an abundance; but whoever does not have, even what he has shall be taken away from him"* (Matt. 13:12). The Savior had begun to speak to them in parables. Upon being asked why He was using parables, He replied, *"To you it has been given to know the mysteries of the kingdom of heaven, but to them it has not been given"* (Matt. 13:11). The unbelieving Jews who had been faithless with the revelation that was given them would be given no further opportunity for light. Christ would hide the truth from them and take away their very capacity to believe.

"For whoever has, to him more shall be given; and whoever does not have, even what he has shall be taken away from him" (Mark 4:25). Obviously he that *"does not have"* had something, otherwise, he could lose nothing. But he did not have what he should have had. This is shown more clearly in the parable of the talents, in Matthew 25:14-30, at the close of which Jesus again repeats, *"For to everyone who has, more shall be given, and he will have an abundance; but from the one who does not have, even what he does have shall be taken away"* (Matt. 25:29). That which every man has to begin with is the natural ability to believe in human faith. God has endowed all men with intellect and reason, as well as displayed before them His glorious works. These are the ingredients necessary for human faith and they make every man responsible toward God. This human faith of which he is capable is not sufficient to justify him, but neglect of such faith is sufficient to damn him. If he responds rightly to human faith, he will gain justifying faith. If not, he will lose even the capacity to think and reason properly. When that happens, all hope is gone.

Faith dies under disobedience. There is such a thing as dead faith. It has no works and is imperfect, and therefore will save no one (James 2:14-26). Two men built houses. One was likened unto a man who heard the Word of God, believed, and obeyed (Matt. 7:24-27). He is said to have built a house upon a rock that withstood the storms of testing.

The other is likened unto a man who heard the words of the Lord and did not obey them. He is said to have built a house upon the sand, and when the storm was over he had nothing left. Both men had something to start with. One was neglectful in what he heard and he did not escape. He lost all that he had at the same time the other was becoming more soundly anchored in the rock.

Men cannot remain static. They must either gain or lose. They progress forward in this great salvation or they digress backward to their ultimate damnation. The servant who was given five talents gained five more and was commended by the Lord. The servant who was given two talents gained two more and was blessed by his master. The servant who did nothing lost all and was rejected by his Lord. Faith always moves from faith to faith. But neglect stops us short and further progress is blocked.

We want to now outline this great salvation as seen in five levels of faith: Human Faith, Justifying Faith, Sanctifying Faith, Deliverance Faith, and Warfare Faith.

Human Faith

Human faith is simply believing what God has done. That is what the Jews in John 2:23 did as they believed the works of God which they saw done in Jesus. So did Nicodemus. *"This man came to Jesus by night and said to Him, 'Rabbi, we know that You have come from God as a teacher; for no one can do these signs that You do unless God is with him'"* (John 3:2). In essence, he was saying, "I believe because I *see* your works." Yet Jesus replies, *"Truly, truly, I say to you, unless one is born again he cannot **see** the kingdom of God"* (John 3:3). He might see the works of God, but he cannot see the Kingdom of God.

The *works* of God are displayed to draw our attention to the *Word* of God so that we may know the *ways* of God.

Believing in such works of God is never enough to save us but is enough to make us accountable to believe His Word. Once we have beheld the works of God, we are faced with His Word and His Truth.

We must either believe it or deny it. *"For the wrath of God is revealed from heaven against all ungodliness and unrighteousness of men who suppress the truth in unrighteousness"* (Rom. 1:18). Why? *"Because that which is known about God is evident within them; for God made it evident to them. For since the creation of the world His invisible attributes* (the things Nicodemus could not see), *both His eternal power and divine nature, have been clearly seen, being understood through what has been made* (the things Nicodemus did see), *so that they are without excuse"* (Rom. 1:19-20). Regardless of whether it is the wonders of life, the marvels of the created universe, or the intervention of God in the normal course of nature, all these works of God move us to give earnest attention to His Word. Otherwise we shall never know His ways.

Will the heathen who have never heard the name of Christ ultimately perish? Most assuredly they will. How can God punish them for refusing to believe in a name they have never heard? This is the question often in men's minds. In other words, *"How will they believe in Him whom they have not heard?"* (Rom. 10:14). But those who ask such questions have not finished reading that passage. Did you not continue? There you will find, *"But I say, have they never heard? On the contrary, they have; 'Their voice has gone out into all the earth, and their words to the ends of the world'"* (Rom. 10:18).

The apostle in this passage appeals to Psalm 19, where it is declared that there is no place on earth where man lacks sufficient witness of God to make him accountable to seek, know, and worship Him. The illiterate and ignorant heathen who sees the works of God displayed all about him, honestly faces the wickedness of his heart being condemned by the law of God written on his conscience, and earnestly seeks to know God will certainly be sent a missionary with the message of Jesus Christ.

But if you, O man, who have like testimony before you, yet continue in your sins, preferring to remain ignorant of the true God lest He demand your repentance, have no reason to expect a higher revelation. You would only trample it under your feet as a sow would precious pearls.

If I give six people material sufficient to learn the alphabet, some may apply themselves to it, learn, seek more reading material, and become learned readers. Others may throw away their first foundations. Should those who neglected to learn the ABCs feel discriminated against when I bestow an encyclopedia on their diligent faithful fellows while withdrawing from them that which I originally supplied them? Even so, those who will not respond rightly to the works of God can never receive the Word of God, and those who rebel against the Word of God may never know the ways of God.

Nicodemus flunked the test at the Word. We do not know if he was ever converted, but he certainly was not saved, at least by the point of John 3. He believed the works yet stumbled at the Word, and the last thing Jesus said of him was that he did not believe (John 3:12). The new birth violated his sense of reason. How tragic! Our eyes behold the works of a supernatural God and we readily consent that such works are too wonderful for us to comprehend. But when our minds are presented with a *truth* that likewise transcends our understanding, we want to balk.

Nicodemus wanted to do it himself. "How do I go about that?" In my early foolish years of attempted soul-winning, when people asked me that question, I tried to tell them how. "Just repent and believe," I said, "and when you do that, you will be born again." Of course, I had no Scripture for this, but thought myself obliged to explain what Jesus neglected to do for Nicodemus. Christ gave no instructions! Repentance and faith are the fruit, not the cause, of regeneration. But back to Nicodemus. *"How can a man be born when he is old? Can he enter a second time into his mother's womb and be born?"* (John 3:4). He foolishly forgets that he had nothing to do with his first birth and thinks he is obliged to engineer his second one. The new birth is no commandment to man. It is a declaration of the way of God for salvation. It is all of God.

That is the rub. It is not what man can do, but what God does. The question is not, "Can a man," but "Can God," or more directly, "Will God?" The wind blows where it wishes, and the Spirit moves as He pleases (John 3:8). This is the truth to which we must consent if we are not to neglect human faith.

The continuing theme of full Bible salvation is the sufficiency of God in the face of the ability of man. The Lord demonstrates His power, reveals His goodness in truth, and then faces us with insurmountable obstacles. He makes promises to us and then bids us to take them when it seems impossible for us to do so. It is the way of faith. It is the way of destruction to the human ego. It brings to an end dependency upon the arm of flesh.

The children of Israel were brought out of Egypt to be welcomed into the full salvation of the land of Canaan. But most of them never made it. They were given human faith by the demonstrated miracles performed by God. They saw His works, yet when given His Word that He had already given them the land of Canaan, they would not believe it. *"We are not able to go up against the people, for they are too strong for us"* (Num. 13:31). Their complaint sounds strikingly similar to Nicodemus. "How can a man?" It is the same complaint the sinner cries when faced with the demands of a Holy God upon his depraved nature. His impotence is evident, but the sufficiency of God is not. Unless he takes that step of obedience by thrusting himself upon the mercy of God in faith, he will never know the wonderful ways of God.

"Therefore, just as the Holy Spirit says, 'Today if you hear His voice, do not harden your hearts as when they provoked Me, as in the day of trial in the wilderness, where your fathers tried Me by testing Me, and saw My works for forty years. Therefore I was angry with this generation, and said, They always go astray in their heart, and they did not know My ways'" (Heb. 3:7-10). They saw His works and on that basis should have hearkened to His Word, but they would not, and so they never knew His ways. Human faith dies under disobedience.

Justifying Faith

Where human faith is believing what God has done, justifying faith is believing what God has done *for me*, personally and particularly, in Christ Jesus. It is one thing to believe that Jesus died on the cross, that He arose from the dead, and that God had a particular design and purpose in this death and resurrection. But to believe that God had me in mind and the purpose of the atonement was to reconcile me to Himself? That is another matter altogether. I cannot, of myself, believe that, nor can any unrepentant sinner believe it. It is futile for soul winners to tell individual persons that Jesus died for their sins. In an unrepentant state, they cannot believe it, no matter how earnestly and fervently you reason with them. No one in the Bible ever told an individual sinner that Christ died for him. They only declared that Christ died for sinners and that in view of this, God commands men everywhere to repent.

"But now apart from the Law the righteousness of God has been manifested, being witnessed by the Law and the Prophets, even the

righteousness of God through faith in Jesus Christ for all those who believe; for there is no distinction; for all have sinned and fall short of the glory of God, being justified as a gift by His grace through the redemption which is in Christ Jesus; whom God displayed publicly as a propitiation in His blood through faith, for a demonstration of His righteousness, because in the forbearance of God He passed over the sins previously committed; for the demonstration of His righteousness at the present time, so that He would be just and the justifier of the one who has faith in Jesus" (Romans 3:21-26).

Justification is a term taken from courts of law. It is what happens when a judge presiding in a court of justice faces a criminal with all the evidence against him demanding his punishment and, knowing very well that the man is guilty, pronounces him innocent. That is exactly what God has done in our case. He has justified us, knowing quite well that we were guilty and deserving of eternal punishment.

Now what would you think of a judge who did such things? How would a citizen react to a judge in their court who had a reputation for finding defendants innocent when he knew very well that they were guilty? That is the problem the apostle is dealing with in the passage just quoted: that God can vindicate His righteousness while justifying sinners. How can He do such a thing? He may demonstrate His mercy, kindness, forbearance, and grace in justifying sinners, but how can he be *just* in doing so when justice demands that they be punished? How can He be just and at the same time the justifier of him which believes in Jesus?

Mercy and justice are here at odds with each other. How can they meet without violating each other? How can God implement His mercy in my justification when I stand before Him with justice pointing out all of my sins, with every true witness declaring that I am worthy of death, and absolutely nothing to plead in my defense?

God has found the solution in Christ Jesus. The just Judge of all the earth has, in the Person of His only begotten Son, taken full punishment for all the crimes committed by those who put their trust in Him. He has satisfied the claims of justice against poor helpless sinners, and having done so, is free to justify them according to His abundant mercy.

But how does a sinner believe that God has reconciled him to Himself in Christ Jesus? How can he believe that his sins have been propitiated in the death of Christ? How can he come to a comforting hope that *he* has an interest in the Savior's blood? There is no way he can persuade himself that this is true. All the arguments presented to him by others can only appeal to a decision in his mind, yet his conscience will still be defiled and the guilt burden of his soul will not be lifted. He cannot produce this justifying faith by an act of intellect, emotion, or will.

There is only one thing that he can do in such a condition. If he has truly been brought to see that he is, as God has declared in His Word, a wicked sinner deserving of hell, he can confess that to be true. He must also confess that he has no hope of improving himself so that he will ever be any less deserving of the wrath of God. He must see that there is no way for him to oblige God to receive him. He will likely at this time confess that he has no reason to believe that God would receive such a wicked person as he.

But, if, in spite of all this, he chooses to forsake his sins, to throw down his arms of rebellion, and to cast himself upon the mercy of the Court, then a very wonderful thing begins to happen. Finding himself incapable of justifying faith, he has pleaded the faithfulness of God, and God has responded. God sends forth the Spirit of His Son into the heart of the repentant sinner crying *"Abba! Father!"* (Gal. 4:6). The sin burden is lifted, peace and joy floods his soul, and he, for the first time, sees that God had him particularly in view in the death of His Son. He sees Christ, for the first time, as his substitute, and is filled with love and gratitude for the free gift of salvation.

Justifying faith is not something the sinner is capable of producing within himself, for this would be mere human faith. It would be a sort of meritorious purchase of salvation in which man could boast. But God has excluded all possibility of that in the design of grace. *"For by grace you have been saved through faith, and this not of yourselves, it is the gift of God"* (Eph. 2:8). Justifying faith is the responsive gift of God to the sinner's repentance, which is also granted by God (Acts 11:18; 2 Tim. 2:25).

In essence, it is not the faith of the sinner, but the faithfulness of Christ Himself, whose Spirit has taken abode in the heart of that same sinner. Man *must* believe: he will perish if he does not. He *ought* to believe: only his wickedness prevents it. But when he *does* believe, it is the gracious gift of faith which comes from God alone.

The first true revelation of the beauty and glory of Christ received by man takes place after God has already done a work of regeneration in him. Paul speaks of his conversion as *"when God, who had set me apart from my mother's womb and called me through His grace, was pleased to reveal **His Son in me**"* (Gal. 1:15-16). It is Christ in you that is your hope of glory (Col. 1:27). One cannot have sound hope of salvation until Christ by the Holy Spirit has indwelt him. It is then that the Holy Spirit bears witness with our spirit that we are sons of God (Rom. 8:16). That is justifying faith, and it is wrought by the wonderful grace of God in the heart of the repentant sinner. It brings us into vital union with Christ. Our need has thrust us to Him, He has stamped His seal upon us, and all that Christ is, is ours, for we are one with Him. He is made unto us wisdom, righteousness, sanctification, and redemption (1 Cor. 1:30).

Sanctifying Faith

Human faith is believing what God has done in Christ Jesus. Justifying faith is believing what God has done *for me* in Christ Jesus. We are now ready to consider the third level of faith, which is sanctifying faith. Sanctifying faith is believing what God has done *with me* in Christ Jesus.

Some will object to the idea of sanctification by faith on the basis that we cannot become holy by just believing that we are. There is much more to it than that. There is a sense in which sanctification can be considered at the same time a work of the Word (Eph. 5:26), a work of the Spirit (1 Pet. 1:2), a work of the chastening Father (Heb. 12:5-10), and the responsibility of the believer himself (1 John 3:3).

But all of these Scriptures are not at odds one with another. They all are a part of the Gospel. The Good News of God is to us, and it saves us who believe it to be true. Sanctification is simply a part of this great salvation.

Perhaps this would be the place for us to define what we are talking about when we speak of sanctification. The terms *sanctification* and *holiness* are synonyms: they point to the same reality in the Scriptures. The Bible speaks of two kinds of holiness: imputed and imparted. The first is legal, the second is experimental. The first is perfect and complete, the second is imperfect and yet incomplete. The first belongs to Christ, the second becomes our own through transformation of the renewing of the mind (Rom. 12:2).

At conversion, the point of justifying faith through union with Christ, God imputes to our account the perfect righteousness of the Lord Jesus Christ. He accounts the holiness of our Lord as our own. All that the Lord Jesus Christ is, He lays to our account, making us legally perfect in His sight. That is justification: God pronouncing us innocent when He knows we are guilty apart from Christ. But God then immediately begins a sanctifying work in us that must culminate in His predestined purpose for the redeemed, who will be conformed to the image of His Son (Rom. 8:29).

Let us go back and consider the justifying Judge for a moment. Having paid the penalty for the guilty, He can legally and justly release him. Justice has been satisfied and so he cannot punish him for what he has *done*. But that has not changed in the least what he *is*. Shall the Judge release this man who is still a criminal and who will surely continue his crimes? Can He set him free to steal, plunder, burn, murder, rape, and ruin as he has previously done?

Such an action might be legal at that point, but it is not moral. Although the courts of men may allow for such, God cannot, because God is not only just, He is moral. His Holy nature will not permit Him to justify the sinner and yet leave him a sinner by nature. Not only has he done something *for* the sinner in Christ Jesus: He has done something *with* him.

We must understand that the Gospel is the preaching of the cross. Everything that is good news to the sinner has already taken place in the death and resurrection of the Lord Jesus Christ. The total redemption of man was finished there in one mighty stroke. What *is* today was finished *then*, yet this cannot be ours in experience until we have heard it in the Gospel, and then it will not save us until we believe it.

Paul takes up the continuing sin question in Romans 6:1. There are those, and I mean no reflection upon their integrity or scholarship, who dogmatically affirm that Romans 6 has nothing to say about sanctification, that it only deals with justification. But the first verse of the chapter denies this. It is manifestly taking up the problem of the justified believer's walk in holiness, and how he will deal with continuing sin in his life after he has been justified.

"What shall we say then? Are we to continue in sin so that grace may increase?" (Rom. 6:1). The popular answer to that ques-

tion is "Of course! How can you do otherwise?" If not stated in those blunt terms, it is no less emphatically declared in the historic confession, "We sin daily in word, thought, and deed." I know I am dealing with a sacred cow here and so want to be careful that I am not misunderstood. I am not taking issue with the fact of whether men *do* actually sin daily in word, thought, and deed, but I am taking issue with the advisability of continuously telling them that they are going to, that they cannot help themselves, that they can do nothing about it, and that in essence there is nothing in the cross of Christ to deliver them from the power of sin. Then after men are told these untruths, they are exhorted to stop sinning, to be holy, and to put away all sinful thoughts, intents, and deeds.

How confusing! Since men must sin, and we preach to them that they must not, perhaps we ought to make a list of sins that are permissible and those that are not. Maybe we could prepare a chart with different shades of sin and illustrate to folks just how far they can venture and when they can and must stop.

Once more let me say that I do not want to be misunderstood or misquoted on this point. I am not going to debate the issue of whether men do sin or not. The issue is, *must* they? Are we Christians still bound by the power of sin? Has Christ delivered us from its penalty and yet left us in its power? That is a level of faith where many stall. They believe that God has done *something for them* in Christ Jesus, but do not believe that God has done *something with them* in Christ Jesus. In exactly the measure in which they do not know or do not believe that God has delivered them from the power of sin, they will continue to be defeated by those sins.

What says the Gospel? *"Knowing this, that our old man was crucified with Him, in order that our body of sin might be done away with, so that we would no longer be slaves to sin"* (Rom. 6:6).

The "old man" is the totality of all that we are apart from Christ. It is self with all its wickedness together with its imagined abilities, goodness, and rights. It is the rebel sinner that is the author of all our crimes. It is the incurable criminal that the holy Law of God has condemned to death. That death sentence was executed in the body of the Savior on Calvary: God put me to death in the person of Christ.

The "body of sin" is not the natural body of flesh, blood, and bones. It is the dynamic of flesh, the law of sin in the members (Rom. 7:23). It is the power that wars against subjection to God and all His holy law. The old man is crucified in order that the body of sin might be rendered of no effect. The word "destroy" does not mean to annihilate, but to strip of its power. That is the message of the Gospel concerning the question of continuing sin after we have been justified freely by the Grace of God. We are not made incapable of sin, but the power of sin has been broken.

What else can such passages as these mean? *"He who has died has been justified from sin"* (Rom. 6:7); *"For sin shall not be master over you"* (Rom. 6:14); *"Having been freed from sin"* (Rom. 6:18); *"But now having been freed from sin"* (Rom. 6:22). That such passages have no reference to the legal consequences of sin but the power of it in the believer's walk is seen by the usages of such words as *serve* or *slave* (Rom. 6:6), *reign* (Rom. 6:12), *obey* (Rom. 6:12), *yield* or *present* (Rom. 6:13), as well as *dominion* or *master* (Rom. 6:14). These words refer to the power and dominion of the sin principle in the believer, and they declare that God has set us free from it through His great salvation in the Lord Jesus Christ on the cross.

That is the Gospel of our sanctification. Can you believe it? If you can, the power is there to save you from continuing sin. However, if you do not believe it, it will do nothing for you, although the work is already finished in Christ Jesus.

All faith is called upon to believe what God has done in the past, yet at the same time, it must relate that finished work to a present reality. It is a futile and useless faith that believes in a God in the past and a God in the future, but which cannot believe Him in the present.

They that come to God must believe that He *is* and that He *is* a rewarder of them that diligently seek him (Heb. 11:6). Modern dispensationalists are the counterparts of the Pharisees of Jesus' day. They believed in the God of Moses and the Prophets. That was past. They believed in the Messiah of the future. Both of these were out of the range of the present. The trouble they had was with the God of the present, Jesus Christ, whom they now faced.

Your faith in the person and reward of God must be brought to the present. It is indicated in the verb "is" in Romans 6:6 in the King James Bible. Now there are those who would argue that this verb should have been translated as "was" since it indicates something that has been completed in the past. I have no argument with that, because the crucifixion of our Lord was a once-for-all completed event. By one offering He has perfected forever those who are sanctified (Heb. 10:14). All that happened when Christ died is complete forever. But since He was crucified, His crucifixion still stands. And since we *were* crucified *with* Him, our crucifixion *is* still a fact. What was slain then *is* still dead. There was a new man raised up with Him to live in resurrection power, but the old man who was executed *is* still in the tomb. God will never resurrect him.

Human reasoning stumbles over the fact that we were put to death in Christ Jesus before we were born, as articulated in the title of L.E. Maxwell's classic book, *Born Crucified*. But this is because we are accustomed to thinking in terms of time and sequence, and God never does. All that shall ever transpire in time was completed by Him in eternity. Therefore He can expiate our sins in Christ before we have committed them. He is the Lamb that was slain before the foundation of the world (1 Pet. 1:19-20; Rev. 13:8). If you have been brought to believe that Christ died for your sins when they were all in the future, is it too difficult a step to believe that you died in Christ before you lived in the flesh?

"Therefore, just as through one man sin entered into the world, and death through sin, and so death spread to all men, because all sinned" (Rom. 5:12). All the human race was present in Adam when he sinned. You were there, and share in the death sentence passed by the holy Law of God. Men now justified were executed in Christ Jesus. You were there, receiving the execution of that death sentence. You do not remember either of those events. But that does not make them any less of a fact. You do not remember your conception in the womb or your natural birth, but they are no less real. You now experience the life that was born, but it existed before you experienced it or believed it.

There is a difference, however, that makes the analogy of the natural to the spiritual imperfect. We *experience* natural life and consequently believe it. But we must *believe* in the spiritual work before it can become an experimental reality. How can a man do this? Once again the impossibility of faith presents itself. Regardless of the record of God's Word, the ability to reckon with what He has said escapes us. We must be shut up and pressed into this level of faith by need, by desperation, and by the requirements God makes of us which we are totally unable to fulfill. As Christ was revealed to us in the Gospel as our sin-bearer, He will be revealed to us in the same Gospel as our sin-deliverer through co-crucifixion.

This revelation does not come until the heart, being set on complete obedience to Christ, and being exceedingly grieved with its failure and disobedience, cries with the frustrated apostle, *"Wretched man that I am! Who will deliver me from the body of this death?"* (Rom. 7:24). He has found himself utterly incapable of subduing the "body of sin." It keeps crying out for its rights, its desires, its pleasures, and though justified man delights in the law of God after the inward man, he cannot consistently obey it.

It is then that the Gospel declaration comes through to him. *"Now those who belong to Christ Jesus crucified the flesh with its passions and desires"* (Gal. 5:24). Dead men have no rights, privileges, or desires. They have no power to demand anything. We discover that we have been foolishly catering to the whims of a dead man. Find a dead man lying in a coffin, walk up to him, and begin insulting him and slapping his face around. See if he comes back fighting like you do when the same happens to you. There it is. That is the only condition under which we can peacefully obey the commands of the Sermon on the Mount. There is not a man alive who can take such abuse and bless, but I am not talking about a man alive. I am talking about a man, dead in Christ, crucified with Him.

But that is only half the story, the negative half. Victory is not in death but in life. Crucifixion puts away the old, but resurrection brings forth the new. And as sure as our crucifixion with Christ is, so is our resurrection. *"Now if we died with Christ, we believe that we shall also live with Him"* (Rom. 6:8). Not only must Adam die, but Christ must live. As God put all of Adam, including me, to death in Christ, so He brought all of Christ, including me, up from the grave to live in the newness of life. It is the dead Adam that will not retaliate when cursed, but the risen Christ that does good to those who hate Him. It is the dead Adam who does not protest when compelled to go the mile, but the risen Christ who goes the second. It is the dead Adam that does not protest God's holy Law, but the risen Christ that delights in His commandments. It is the dead Adam who no longer cries for the fleshpots of Egypt, but the risen Christ who delights in the milk and honey of Canaan, the unseen spiritual realities, the heavenly things of the Lord.

What has happened as this begins to characterize the life of the believer? Has he acquired something that he did not have before? A special separate work of grace? A second blessing? A state of entire sanctification? Has he been filled with the Spirit?

Many terms are used that have varying degrees of validity, but the fact is, the believer has nothing more than he had when he was justified. Justification is Christ in the believer for his justification by faith. Sanctification is Christ in the believer for his sanctification. His sanctification begins to become real to him in experience as he begins to believe and reckon all that Christ is instead of all that he himself is not. He is no longer limited by what he is but by what Christ is in him. And Christ is in the believer for all things that pertain to life and godliness. Therefore God will never make any demands upon the believer for which He has not supplied that sufficiency in the indwelling Christ. Nothing has been added since justification except faith, and more specifically sanctifying faith. Through the Gospel the righteousness of God in making holy people of wretched sinners through the cross of Christ is revealed, and men, in beholding, are transformed from glory to glory.

Deliverance Faith

We are now ready to consider the fourth level of faith: deliverance faith. Human faith is believing what God has done in Christ Jesus. Justifying faith is believing what God has done *for me* in Christ Jesus. Sanctifying faith is believing what God has done *with me* in Christ Jesus. Deliverance faith is believing what God does *in me* in Christ Jesus. *"Who rescued us from the authority of darkness, and transferred us to the kingdom of the Son of His love"* (Col. 1:12-13).

It was a great victory for the devil when the Christian church began to leave demonology out of soteriology. Every book that has been written on sanctification, as great a blessing as they have been up to a point, has fallen short because the writer has ignored the dynamic of evil spiritual powers of darkness. The cry is constantly made against the flesh, the flesh, the flesh! Yet the Word of God plainly declares that we wrestle not against flesh and blood, but against principalities, against powers, against the rulers of the darkness of this world, against spiritual wickedness in high places (Eph. 6:12). The flesh, the body of flesh and blood, is not inherently evil, but neutral. Evil does not exist in things but in spiritual principles.

There is a natural propensity toward sin in fallen man, in the old unconverted nature, but it is a weak fallen power. Jesus declared that the flesh is weak (Matt. 26:41). We are not being overcome by our flesh but by an evil principle *in* the flesh. Paul never cries out against the flesh in Romans 7:17-21: *"So now, no longer am I the one working it out, but sin which dwells **in** me. For I know that nothing good dwells **in** me, that is, **in** my flesh; for the willing is present **in** me, but the working out of the good is not. For the good that I want, I do not do, but I practice the very evil that I do not want. But if I am doing the very thing I do not want, I am no longer the one working it out, but sin which dwells **in** me. I find then the principle that **in** me evil is present—**in** me who wants to do good."* There is an evil dynamic in him overcoming and causing him to sin that is not him. Yet he is not absolving himself of personal responsibility, for he confesses: *"I am fleshly, having been sold into bondage under sin"* (Rom. 7:14).

The flesh is involved in all sin and is the *occasion* of the bondage of man to sin, but the flesh is not the *power*. That power is a demonic power, meaning principalities and rulers of the darkness of this world. Paul found his victory in Christ Jesus, as all believers must. *"Thanks be to God through Jesus Christ our Lord!"* (Rom. 7:25).

Demonic powers have been recognized and dealt with usually in extreme cases involving the occult. But we must, if we are to have real and lasting victory, recognize that the working of demons is not so limited. Did not a third part of the angels join Satan in his rebellion against God (Rev. 12:4, Rev. 12:9)? Then what are these fallen spirits doing? Sitting around twiddling their thumbs? You may be assured they are not. Then in whom are they working?

First, we should say that demons work in *all* unbelievers. *"You formerly walked according to the course of this world, according to the ruler of the power of the air, the spirit that is now working **in** the sons of disobedience"* (Eph. 2:2). The prince of the power of the air is Satan. His "spirit" is the multitude of demon spirits who work in unconverted sinners. Why should they not? Demons desire men to worship them by doing their will. They desire to have bodies in which to exercise their wicked natures. The lost sinner has absolutely no defenses against demonic forces. They can come and go as they please because the sinner is still under the power and rule of darkness. He belongs to the family of Satan, the kingdom and authority of darkness (John 8:44).

But are not Christians immediately and automatically delivered from these powers when they trust in Christ? No, they are not. But the objection is made that the Scriptures plainly declare that He has delivered us. How could we still be bound if He has already delivered us? We can find the same terminology in relation to justification and sanctification. *"Therefore do not be ashamed of either the witness about our Lord or me His prisoner, but join with me in suffering for the gospel according to the power of God, who has saved us and called us with a holy calling, not according to our works, but according to His own purpose and grace which was given to us in Christ Jesus from all eternity"* (2 Tim. 1:8-9).

God had already saved all who would be saved before the world began. Must not unconverted people then be saved since they already are in the eternal finished work of Christ? Indeed they must or they will surely perish! *"For by one offering He has perfected for all time those who are being sancti-fied"* (Heb. 10:14). Must not men be sanctified since they were in the finished work of Christ on the cross? Indeed they must! The works of God were finished from the foundation of the world, but we must be brought to experimentally partake of those finished works if we are to derive benefit from them. We become what God has already made us in Christ Jesus by believing the fact of it and reckoning with it. Until then, it is of no consequence to us, although the works were indeed finished (Heb. 4:3).

In like fashion, God has delivered us from the power of the devil, but it will be of no avail to us until we believe it. Satan is a legalist when the law is on his side. He will demand and claim all that is within his power to possess and rule. But when the law is against him, he is an outlaw. The whole tenor of his person is lawlessness. He is in constant defiance of God's law.

Though the death and resurrection of Christ have rendered him subject to the believer rather than the believer to him, he will still hold dominion over the child of God unless that child of God believes the Gospel. The portion of the Gospel that he must believe at this point has to do with the victory of Christ *on our behalf* over the powers of darkness. We must not forget that any victory Christ won over the devil had to be on our behalf since Satan has never had any dominion over Christ. All that Christ did in relation to the devil and demons has our personal victory in view.

What does the Gospel say? *"Having disarmed the rulers and authorities, He made a public display of them, having triumphed over them in Him"* (Col. 2:15). He completely robbed them of their power over those who shared in His death and resurrection. *"What is the surpassing greatness of His power toward us who believe according to the working of the might of His strength, which He worked in Christ, by raising Him from the dead and seating Him at His right hand in the heavenly places, far above all rule and authority and power and dominion, and every name that is named, not only in this age but also in the one to come. And He put all things in subjection under His feet... and raised us up with Him, and seated us with Him in the heavenly places in Christ Jesus"* (Eph. 1:19-22, Eph. 2:6). God has put every creature, angel, man, and beast in heaven, hell, and earth under the feet of Jesus. Then He raised us up to sit in that exalted position in Christ. If demons are then under the feet of Christ, they are also under ours!

Will you believe it, dear friend? If you do not, it does not change the fact of the matter. *"If we are faithless, He remains faithful, for He cannot deny Himself"* (2 Tim. 2:13). But the facts of the Gospel will be of no benefit to you until you believe them, because the Gospel saves believers.

It would be only fair to say at this point that many cannot believe in this level of faith because they have balked at some prior level. Only those who respond rightly to human faith can know anything of justifying faith. It is no good to attempt to lay hold of sanctifying faith if you have not yet been justified, and no one can consistently lay hold of deliverance faith if they have not obtained a solid grasp of sanctifying faith.

The occasion of demonic powers is flesh. Uncrucified flesh provides the beachhead for this enemy to invade the man. Before a man has a demonic problem, he has a flesh problem. This is always the case. Much of the quibbling about whether some phenomenon is fleshly or demonic is a waste of time. It is usually both in some measure.

Is idolatry and witchcraft, for example, demonic or fleshly? If we could say with certainty that anything is demonic, it would have to be idolatry and witchcraft. These phenomena are supernatural to the core. Yet Galatians 5:19-21 lists them among the works of the flesh! *"I am fleshly, having been sold into bondage under sin"* cries the apostle (Rom. 7:14). In that area where flesh rules, the devil has dominion. The flesh opens the door.

Suppose we are sitting in a room with the door open as mosquitoes are swarming around and biting us. Would you say we had a mosquito problem or a door problem? Obviously, we have both. The mosquitoes need to be exterminated, but it will do no lasting good as long as the door remains open. Close the door, swat the mosquitoes, and the problem is solved so long as the door is not again opened. The door of uncrucified flesh must be kept firmly closed before one can know lasting deliverance from the power of demons.

But many have gone this far and yet find themselves in bondage that confession and reckoning on co-crucifixion with Christ will not break. They must recognize that this overwhelming power is not flesh but spirit, demon spirits, and counting on their resurrected position in Christ Jesus, take authority over the particular spirit causing the problem and demand that he leave and never come back. These are the mountains that Jesus said would remove themselves upon our command in faith (Matt. 21:21; Mark 11:23). This is a realm of faith and victory of which too few Christians of this day and age know anything. May the Lord give us grace to believe it.

Warfare Faith

We are now ready to consider a level of faith that few Christians indeed attain. Warfare faith is believing what God does *through* us. As far as I can determine from the study of the Scriptures, since Abraham came upon the scene, God never acted among men apart from the cooperation and intercession of His people. I do not say that He cannot act, but it seems that He does not. *"Surely Lord Yahweh does nothing unless He reveals His secret counsel to His slaves the prophets"* (Amos 3:7).

When the Lord determined to destroy Sodom for her wickedness He said, *"Shall I conceal from Abraham what I am about to do?"* (Gen. 18:17). The answer was an obvious no. The ensuing conversation typifies how God deals with a man in his prayers and intercessions until the man agrees with God on the matter. When Abraham saw that Sodom indeed was worthy of destruction and without remedy, then God proceeded with His purpose.

God appointed priests to stand between Him and the transgressor so that He might deal with them mercifully. He appointed a man, Christ Jesus, to be our eternal Intercessor. He has appointed the means of intercessory prayers and the preaching of the Gospel to facilitate the salvation of sinners. It cannot be demonstrated that anyone was ever soundly converted to Christ for whom someone else had not interceded. Since God only responds to faith, and the unbelieving are incapable of faith, then someone else must believe for those who cannot.

We are talking about vicarious faith. This is a faith that one person has on behalf of someone else. Examples of such faith abound in the Scriptures. Jesus declares the failure of His disciples to be caused by unbelief (Matt. 17:19-20). Our failures on behalf of others are not caused by our not working hard enough, long enough, or skillfully enough, but because of our unbelief.

When a father brought his demon-possessed son to Jesus, the Lord asked the father, not the son, to believe (Mark 9:20-24). The little boy was incapable of faith. He was bound by the demon. It is true of your own loved ones who are lost. They are not free moral agents who can accept Christ at will when a persuasive enough argument is put to them. They are bound immoral prisoners, totally incapable of laying hold on saving faith. Someone must believe God for them so that the power of the devil can be broken on their hearts and minds.

This truth is dramatically demonstrated in Mark 2:1-5. Four men come bearing their paralyzed friend to Jesus. Unable to approach Christ through the normal route, the door, they climbed onto the roof, took up the tiling, and lowered the sick man down into the room. *"Jesus seeing **their** faith said to the paralytic, 'Child, your sins are forgiven.'"* What sort of theology is that? We can safely say it is Biblical theology and one that is every bit practical. The sins of a man are forgiven because of the faith of others! And it is a principle that we dare not ignore. If we are to wage an effectual warfare for the souls of men, we must believe God *for* them.

Now comes the next logical question. For whom am I responsible for believing God? Can I believe Him for anyone at will? If so, why not for everyone in my community, my city, my state, and the whole world? If such a thing were possible, it would only be so theoretically, because it has never been demonstrated. No one has ever done it. Nor do we have any spiritual grounds to say someone should have. But we are responsible for believing God for *someone*. Then who is it? How can one know for whom he is to intercede, for whom he is to spare nothing for their salvation, for whom he is to risk all until he presents them to Christ?

The answer to these questions may be found in Jesus' parable of the persistent friend in Luke 11:5-8:

"Then He said to them, 'Which of you has a friend and will go to him at midnight and say to him, "Friend, lend me three loaves, for a friend of mine has come to me from a journey, and I have nothing to set before him"; and from inside he answers and says, "Do not bother me; the door has already been shut and my children and I are in bed; I cannot rise up and give you anything." I tell you, even though he will not arise and give him anything because he is his friend, yet because of his persistence he will get up and give him as much as he needs.'"

We must notice that this man was asking nothing for himself. He was interceding on behalf of the need of another person. We must also notice that his success was not due to his good standing with his friend. *"He will not arise and give him anything because he is his friend."* He is not pleading on the basis of his friendship or anything his neighbor may owe him. He is pleading solely on the basis of his *utter inability to supply the needs of another person for which he has found himself responsible.*

As with all parables, this must be interpreted into spiritual realities. Someone is standing on your doorstep crying for bread. Bread is a type of Christ. He is the bread of which man eats and lives forever (John 6:51). Do you have anything within yourself to feed them? Can you supply their need? Can you save them? Can you deliver them from the power of darkness?

If you think you can, my friend, then you are surely deluded. Only God can meet the needs of those for whom you have become responsible. Can you believe God to meet them? Are there grounds for your faith on their belief? Yes! Yes! Yes! The highest and soundest grounds that exist. For if someone is on your doorstep crying for bread, you can be assured that God sent them there; and He did not send them there to mock you. He sent them there to drive you in desperation to Him that they might be saved!

What are you going to do about those three little children He has put in your home? Surely you are not going to mope around wondering if they are elect or not. Get busy campaigning for them. He charged you with the responsibility to train them in the nurture and admonition of the Lord. You are to watch for their souls. They may not now appear so to you, but they are just as mean as any man who ever lived. They will lie, cheat, steal, hate, fight, slander, and do everything that any and all of the fallen race of Adam will do. And you cannot stop them. Surely you can love them, discipline them, and teach them while they are at home and in your sight. But you cannot watch them all the time.

Someday they will leave home and then they will really be what they are, not what you force them to be. If God does not save them, they have the potential of becoming the worst sort of criminal. It may so be that you will have impressed strong enough social restraints upon them that they will become polished hypocrites and respected church members, only to die and go to hell.

Is it coming across, dear friend? You do not have any bread. You are bankrupt. If God does not intervene, you are sunk. *You have to trust Him.*

What we have said about your children may well apply to any person to whom you have the opportunity to minister, whether that is a relative, spouse, neighbor, business acquaintance, or fellow worker. It could be anyone who in some way is looking to you for bread. If you can believe, all things are possible for him that believes (Mark 9:23). It is only fair to say that there will be some for whom you cannot believe. It does not mean that they are non-elect. It simply means you cannot believe for them. But there are some for which you *must* believe. Do it! It is the highest motivation you will ever have to believe God.

Insights from Christendom

"He who is called must go out of his situation in which he cannot believe, into the situation in which, first and foremost, faith is possible. But this step is not the first stage of a career. Its sole justification is that it brings the disciple into fellowship with Jesus which will be victorious. So long as Levi sits at the receipt of custom, and Peter at his nets, they could both pursue their trade honestly and dutifully, and they might both enjoy religious experiences, old and new. But if they want to believe in God, the only way is to follow His incarnate Son.

Unless a definite step is demanded, the call vanishes into thin air, and if men imagine that they can follow Jesus without taking this step, they are deluding themselves like fanatics.

Only the obedient can believe. If we are to believe we must obey a concrete command. Without this preliminary step of obedience, our faith will only be pious humbug."

DIETRICH BONHOEFFER

Meditating on the Word

Read and reflect on Genesis 12:1-4, John 1:16, Romans 1:17, and 2 Corinthians 3:18.

Questions for Reflection

1. What are the five levels of faith, and can you briefly describe each one?
2. What is meant by vicarious faith? (Refer to Matt. 17:19-20; Mark 9:23; Luke 11:5-8)
3. What is faith called to believe and do?
4. How does believing in God and experiencing natural realities differ from believing in and experiencing spiritual realities?
5. What insights about faith has God revealed to you in this chapter?

For Further Reading

Read *Of God and Men* by A.W. Tozer.

FAITH COMETH

"Therefore, do not throw away that confidence of yours, which has a great reward. For you have need of endurance, so that when you have done the will of God, you may receive the promise. For yet in a very little while, He who is coming will come, and will not delay. But My righteous one shall live by faith, and if he shrinks back, My soul has no pleasure in him. But we are not of those who shrink back to destruction, but of those who have faith to the preserving of the soul. Now faith is the assurance of things hoped for, the conviction of things not seen. For by it the men of old gained approval" (Hebrews 10:35-11:2).

A STUDY of faith is usually begun with Hebrews 11:1. But if we begin there, we miss the tone of urgency that is set in the closing verses of Hebrews 10.

The Ultimate End of Faith

Make no mistake about it. Hebrews 11 is not an exposition on a handy accessory to the Christian life that tells us how to believe God and get what we want out of Him. It has nothing less than justification and full salvation in view all the way through.

The phrase *"gained approval,"* and in some translations *"obtained a good report,"* in Hebrews 11:2 and 11:39 is translated from the Greek word *martureo*. It is translated elsewhere in the New Testament as *"bear record"* thirteen times, *"bear witness"* twenty-five times, and *"testify"* nineteen times. It is the same word used of Abel in Hebrews 11:4: *"He was approved as being righteous."* The faith toward which the writer of Hebrews is urging us is the faith that brought witness and testimony of the *righteousness* by which God has justified and received the Old Testament saints. That is the good report that they obtained and the approval they gained.

That is the end toward which we are urged to persevere in the closing verses of chapter 10. *"Do not throw away that confidence." "You have need of endurance." "For yet in a very little while." "My righteous one shall live by faith." "We are not of those who shrink back."*

Perseverance is the dominating part of faith from the side of man, so much so that we can almost say that perseverance *is* faith, but we cannot, for that would make faith man-centered.

We must understand that faith is linear, progressive, dynamic, moving, and looking toward rather than stationary, static, past, and settled. It always has the ultimate salvation of the soul as its future end: "Those who have faith to the preserving of the soul." While promises along the way of lesser blessings may be received or not received, the salvation of the soul is ever in view. In Hebrews 11 we are told of many who through faith *received*, but then we are told of some who *"received not the promise"* (Heb. 11:39), yet obtained the good report, gaining approval of justification in the sight of God because of their perseverance in faith.

In true Bible faith, the possibility of apostasy is never

forgotten and the warning of the sure consequence of eternal perdition is ever before us. It is manifest that some do draw back into perdition (Heb. 10:39), but we must make sure that we are of them who believe to the saving of the soul.

Having now put in the right perspective the purpose of Hebrews 11, we will consent that along the way of faith we are encouraged by receiving certain blessings that God has promised us. The presence of these does encourage us, but the absence or scarcity of them must never be allowed to discourage us and turn us from trusting God.

What Is Faith?

No one can provide an exhaustive and conclusive definition of faith. There are several ways we can describe faith, but none of them will sufficiently define faith. We have already stated that faith is something you do in view of Who God is and in response to what He said.

Hebrews 11:1 gives another look at what faith is. Many have been the expositions of this verse, but its meaning is still obscure to the average Christian layman. We are told two things that faith is: substance or *assurance*, and evidence or *conviction*. The substance is of things hoped for but not yet received, and the evidence is of things that are not yet seen.

The Greek word translated as substance means *substratum*, or the underlying support. It is that which gives grounds and support to a thing. The Greek word translated as evidence in the King James and conviction in the Legacy Standard is *elegchos*, translated elsewhere as "reproof." Its related root *elegcho* is translated elsewhere in the New Testament as "convict" once, "convince" four times, "reprove" six times, and "rebuke" five times. *Elegcho* is the same word used in John 16:8 where it says of the Holy Spirit, *"And He, when*

He comes, will **convict** the world concerning sin and righteousness and judgment."

The word means to so impress upon the heart and mind the truth of the matter so as to cause him to commit himself and his actions to that truth. Putting that together we have the following paraphrase: *"Faith is the underlying support and basis of the things for which we have hope, and is that which convinces us they are true even though no visible or tangible evidence exists."*

Now let us demonstrate this through one example of faith in the Bible. It is called little faith, but it is faith nonetheless. Matthew 14:25-31 records an incident when Peter walked on water. When Peter stepped out of that boat and onto the water, what was the substratum under his feet? The water would not support him. What did hold him up? It was nothing less than the Word of God, the invitation of Jesus to "Come." What convinced and persuaded him to leave the boat and stand upon the water? There was no evidence of anything there to support him. It was not because of past experiences in walking on water. What then convinced him? The same thing that supported him in the act of faith, the Word of God, in this case the command of Christ to come.

Nothing else can convince and nothing else can support. The same word that convinces is the word that supports. Faith that comes from God is supported by God. If anything else other than God and His Word gives corroborative or supportive evidence, or if we are depending on something or someone other than God to support us in our act of faith, then it is not pure faith. *"He who draws near to God must believe that He is and that He is a rewarder of those who seek Him"* (Heb. 11:6). Most everyone believes in the first "is," that is, the existence of God. But how difficult it is to believe in the second "is." He is now presently my rewarder, my support, my strength, and my salvation.

How Faith Comes

How does a man come by this faith? How does he lay hold upon it? How does he come to believe that God is his rewarder? You may read dozens of books and pamphlets and listen to hundreds of sermons that will tell you how to acquire faith, to believe God, to turn your faith loose, or to exercise your latent faith.

They are all lies! Nowhere in the Scriptures are we told any of these. We are commanded to believe God. We are told that *if* we have faith nothing will be impossible for us, but we are never told in the Bible how to acquire that faith. It is foolish and ignorant men who tell you that. If what they were saying were true, if it indeed would work as they assure you it would, then that secret would have been common knowledge a long time ago, and everybody would be exercising that faith by working miracles, creating new worlds, and everything that God alone can do.

Faith cannot be initiated from the human side. How shall we recognize a situation in which it is possible for us to believe God from purely human emotion, will, or intellect?

Not by human emotion. Human desires cannot be trusted. They are too easily inflamed by the devil and too often these are simply the cryings of our fallen nature. *"You ask and do not receive, because you ask with wrong motives, so that you may spend it on your pleasures"* (James 4:3). Even apparently noble evangelical undertakings may simply be appealing to our religious pride.

Not by human will. Least of all this! "I will" is the very essence of sin. This was the cry of Lucifer in his rebellion against God. *"But you said in your heart, 'I will ascend to heaven; I will raise my throne above the stars of God, and I will sit on the mount of assembly in the recesses of the north. I will ascend above the heights of the clouds; I will make myself like the Most High'"*

(Isa. 14:13-14). It is throwing off the will of God and substituting self-will. Too often we have convinced ourselves that the strong "I will" is the will of God. Not so! The man who bends to the will of God does it in meek submission, not in aggressive defiance. You cannot conjure faith by a strong assertion of the will.

Not by the virtue in the thing. Hundreds of potential deeds have great virtue in them. Which deed does God want you to do? Manifestly you cannot do all of them, so it cannot be His Will for you to do them all. What is the one thing He wants you to do in faithful obedience? There are six hundred million starving pagans in India. There are two thousand dialects with no Bible and no Gospel in the dark extremities of human habitation. Scotland and England, once the home bases of world evangelism, have now become apostate and need to be evangelized once more. America has long become pagan. Your own community has orphanages and nursing homes where elderly people are dying and slipping into hell. Work in any of these areas would be greatly virtuous, but does that alone make it a work of faith?

Let us assume for a moment that the virtue of a thing would make it a work of faith and that God would honor it as such and let us presume a course of action on that basis. Since everyone seems to believe that Jesus is coming soon and that millions will go to hell if they are not saved, then it is sheer foolishness to continue working on a job and earning money to buy food, clothing, shelter, and electricity. We should all quit our jobs tomorrow, sell our possessions, give to the poor, buy a sack of tracts and Bibles, and start evangelizing. Will not God honor that? Did He not tell us to go into all the world and preach the Gospel? Are not the cattle on a thousand hills His? Then let us go. What are you waiting for?

"Ah," you say, "I don't have any faith." "Nonsense," I reply.

"Turn your faith loose. Put God on the spot. Obligate Him to take care of you." But all of my foolish arguments will not produce one iota of faith in you. And without faith, you had better continue on your job, and as the Scriptures say, *"Attend to your own business and work with your hands, just as we commanded you, so that you will walk properly toward outsiders and not be in any need"* (1 Thess. 4:11-12).

Not by sheer urgency. Faith cannot be initiated simply because our intellect tells us that a situation is so desperate that God has to do something. You come upon an automobile wreck. Three people are dying in it. You see broken bones, crushed chests, and blood gushing out of ripped arteries. Alcohol is everywhere. The three are lost and they will be in hell in fifteen minutes if something does not happen. Can you believe God to heal them all immediately so that they can be saved? Can you prevail upon God to give them consciousness and saving faith so that they may be converted before they die? Where are all these "healing" evangelists who claim that it is always the will of God to heal? Surely one of these would have enough faith to do this, don't you think? Your neighbor's house is on fire. Why do you not just believe God to send a downpour and put it out? Did Elijah not believe God for rain? Was he not a man just like you? Then why can you not do it?

There is an answer to all of these questions. Faith cannot be produced or initiated from the human side. You do not have it to turn loose, and you cannot get it. It comes from God at His prerogative alone.

"So faith comes from hearing, and hearing by the word of Christ" (Rom. 10:17). If this passage read as it is generally understood, it would read like this. *"Faith comes by hearing the Word of God."* For we are told that the more preaching one listens to, the more Bible he reads, then the more faith he will have. Such may be true in some cases, but certainly not

in all. Multitudes have sat in church for years listening to sound Bible truth and have not an ounce of faith. Others, having taught Sunday School for years, have spent long hours with their Bible, and yet know nothing of faith. Why? Because although they have "listened" and read, they have never "heard" and have never "seen."

To understand Romans 10:17, we must carefully consider the "so" with which the verse begins. This word points us to consideration of the immediately preceding verses.

Romans 10:13 is also frequently quoted out of context as a formula for salvation: *"Whoever calls on the name of the Lord will be saved."* Upon this "promise," any man at any time under any conditions is urged to call upon the Lord to save him. That many do so call and are not subsequently saved is a fact that anyone knows well if he has ever attempted this sort of evangelism. They are not saved because there has been no faith in the call. This "promise" is immediately followed by four "How wills" which will always qualify a call upon the Lord in saving faith. Let us consider these "How wills" in Romans 10:14-15.

*"**How** then **will** they call on Him in whom they have not believed?"* Obviously, many do call in unbelief, but it is not a call according to Romans 10:13.

*"**How will** they believe in Him whom they have not heard?"* Obviously, they cannot.

*"**How will** they hear without a preacher?"* This is the absolute necessity of human instrumentality.

*"**How will** they preach unless they are sent?"* Ah! Have not many found ways to do this? Are not many uncalled preachers preaching? Most assuredly yes. But the hearing of faith will not accompany their preaching. Before one can savingly call upon the Lord, he must call upon the One of whom he has heard by the voice of a God-sent preacher.

That preacher is sent by the *Word* of God. So then faith cometh by hearing and hearing by the *Word* of God.

Many hear and hear, yet do not hear, because they have not yet received the hearing ear. To every one of the seven churches in Asia of Revelation 2 and Revelation 3, the Spirit speaks three things: *"I know your deeds," "He who has an ear, let him hear what the Spirit says to the churches,"* and *"He who overcomes, I will."* Obviously the Spirit is not addressing Himself to everyone, but only to those who have the hearing ear. Jesus used the same qualification many times. *"He who has ears to hear, let him hear"* (Matt.11:15).

The natural faculty is not in view here, or else God would be excluding only those who are physically deaf. It is a spiritual ear, an ability to receive intuitive communication from God that is indicated. *"But just as it is written, 'Things which eye has not seen and ear has not heard, and which have not entered the heart of man, all that God has prepared for those who love Him.' But to us God* **revealed** *them through the Spirit, for the Spirit searches all things, even the depths of God"* (1 Cor. 2:9-10). This is a direct reference to Isaiah 64:4: *"For from ancient times they have not heard or given ear, nor has the eye seen a God besides You, Who acts in behalf of the one who waits for Him."*

We do not hear the Word of God by the outer hearing faculty, nor do we see spiritual realities by the natural eye, nor do we receive them by the "heart" or natural emotions. God is a Spirit and He always communicates with us spiritually.

This is not to set aside the importance of the preaching of the word by human instrumentality. Two witnesses are given: the witness from without through the preached Word and the written Scriptures, and the witness within by the Holy Spirit. But the witness without can never provide the evidence of things hoped for and the convincing that is needed to cause one to commit himself to that truth. The

Holy Spirit alone in communication with the human spirit can do that.

This hearing ear comes from the creative Word of God, the revelation of His Arm of salvation. *"Who has believed our report? And to whom has the arm of Yahweh been revealed?"* (Isa. 53:1). This is a literary device in which two questions are asked, and the answer of the first is contained in the second. Who believes? He to whom the arm of the Lord is revealed. That is creative hearing by the Word of God. This passage is quoted in John 12:38 and again in Romans 10:16, both in the context of the ability or inability of man to hear and believe. *"The hearing ear and the seeing eye, Yahweh has made both of them"* (Prov. 20:12).

Second Mention Basics of Faith

The second time we have faith mentioned in the Bible is Habakkuk 2:1-4, from which we will glean some further basics of faith. First of all, from the context, we find that an opportunity for faith comes during adversities and perplexities. The prophet could not understand why God was not doing something. The law is slacked. Judgment and justice have not gone forth. The wicked have trodden down the righteous. How can God look on such evil when He is so pure? Why does God not consume these idolaters who worship their nets?

Eventually Habakkuk makes a wise decision: *"I will stand on my guard post and station myself on the fortification; And I will keep watch to see what He will speak to me and how I may respond when I am reproved. Then Yahweh answered me and said, 'Write down the vision and write it on tablets distinctly, that the one who reads it may run. For the vision is yet for the appointed time; It pants toward its end, and it will not lie. Though it tarries, wait for it; For it will certainly come; it will not delay. Behold, as for the proud one, His soul is not right within him; But the righteous will live by his faith'"* (Hab. 2:1-4).

Stop complaining about the situation you are in and railing against God because He has not done anything yet. You cannot make God answer you, so stop trying. Sit down and wait for Him to speak. If you cannot remedy the situation and you cannot make God do it, then there is nothing else for you to do. Wait for Him to speak to you and be prepared to respond, for you must do something when He speaks. He *will* speak.

When God speaks, you have your basis for faith. You can "write the vision" and engrave it upon tables of stone. It will not have to be erased and revised tomorrow, next year, or in a thousand millennia. The Word of God is as immutable as He is. What He said ten thousand years ago is just as fresh and dependable as the day it was uttered. Who could want a better *substratum* of things hoped for?

Whoever reads this word must "run." When the word comes, a commitment must be made to it. You cannot act until the word comes, but when it does come, you must act. To not act is dead faith and useless. Here is human responsibility at its critical point. There will be no other reason or incentive for you to act except the "vision." But that will be sufficient. Again we say that *faith is something you do in view of Who God is and in response to what He has said.*

Elements in Real Faith

We now want to point out some elements that are always present in real Bible faith. Some of these will seem strange to us, but if what we are calling faith does not have them, then what we have is not real faith.

Doubt: Doubt is not the opposite of faith as some suppose, but a vital element in it. If you have everything wrapped up in a neat package where there can be no possibility of error or slip, as one would say, "a lead pipe cinch," is there any faith in such a thing? If there are no challenges, and no suggestions of failure possible, then it is not faith. Hear the cry of the demonized boy's father: *"I do believe; help my unbelief!"* (Mark 9:24). Was doubt there? It most certainly was. Was it yet faith? Yes. The boy was delivered and Jesus had conditioned the deliverance on the faith of the father. Did the Hebrew children doubt that God would deliver them from the fiery furnace? They certainly did. There was not a note of assurance of deliverance in their answer, only assurance that they intended to trust God whether they were delivered or not. Is that faith? It certainly is. Cast not away your confidence in God because of your doubt. If you continue to follow Him, it is faith nonetheless. Doubts of salvation are common among the genuine children of God, just as false assurance of salvation is common among the disobedient children of the devil.

Fear: *"I heard, and my inward parts trembled; At the sound my lips tingled. Decay enters my bones, and in my place I tremble. Because I must wait quietly for the day of distress, for the people to arise who will invade us"* (Hab. 3:16). Is that a description of a man's fears? It certainly is. Could such a man have faith while in such fear? Yes! Listen to his confession: *"Though the fig tree should not blossom and there be no produce on the vines, though the yield of the olive should fail and the fields yield no food, though the flock should be cut off from the fold and there be no cattle in the stalls, yet I will exult in Yahweh; I will rejoice in the God of my salvation. Yahweh, the Lord, **is** my strength, and He **has** set my feet like hinds' feet and **makes** me tread on my high places"* (Hab. 3:17-19). A greater confession of faith you will find nowhere, and it was made by a man with butterflies in his stomach, his knees knocking, and his limbs as weak as water because of his fear. Do not throw away your faith because you have fear and trembling. Indeed the Lord has admonished us to work out our salvation with fear and trembling. We are extremely skeptical of faith which does not have an element of fear in it.

Choice: *"By faith Moses, when he had grown up, refused to be called the son of Pharaoh's daughter, choosing rather to be mistreated with the people of God than to enjoy the passing pleasures of sin, regarding the reproach of Christ greater riches than the treasures of Egypt; for he was looking to the reward"* (Heb. 11:24-26). We stated that faith cannot be initiated by an act of will, but once it is initiated by God, the will *must* choose. Choice does not produce faith, but faith, when it comes, indeed chooses. See what convincing evidence God must have given Moses through the ear and eye of faith. He was directly in line to the Pharaoh of Egypt, dictator of the mightiest power in the ancient world. He could have allowed himself to be called an Egyptian and become heir to all the treasures of Egypt. But he would not allow himself to be called the son of Pharaoh's daughter because he was the son of Levi's daughter, and although it could not yet be seen with the natural eye, an heir of all the riches of Christ. All that Moses could see with the natural eye was the Egyptian slave camps where the people with whom he chose to identify himself were suffering. You see how powerful this *evidence of things not seen* is. What powerful, persuasive, convincing force it carries! It can tear a man loose from the strongest material, emotional, social, and logical ties on earth. But that man, when faced with such evidence, must himself choose. What are you, dear friend? An Egyptian? If so, you may well enjoy the world. But if not an Egyptian, a spiritual Jew, then you may as well throw your lot in with the people of God, whoever and wherever they are. It is where you belong and where you will find the true riches.

Warfare: *"Who through faith conquered kingdoms, performed righteousness, obtained promises, shut the mouths of lions, quenched the power of fire, escaped the edge of the sword, were made strong from weakness, became mighty in war, put foreign armies to flight"* (Heb. 11:33-34). No matter how peaceable and congenial you may be, when you commit yourself to a life of faith, you have declared war. The enemy will surely challenge you on every side. He will threaten you with the loss of everything you hold dear. He will promise you material, social, and religious ruin, and will do everything in his power to make his promise good. You will be beset by fears and doubts, obstacles and perplexities, disappointments and treachery everywhere you turn. But all of this cannot shake the pure and perfect end of your faith one bit. It is anchored solidly in the Person and Word of Almighty God. You cannot possibly lose the battle. Unchallenged faith is worthless, and a victorious warfare of faith is priceless.

Delay: *"For the vision is yet for the appointed time; It pants toward its end, and it will not lie. Though it tarries, wait for it; For it will certainly come; it will not delay"* (Hab. 2:3). You must wait for God to speak. When He speaks and you respond, you must then wait for the promise. Though there is a delay, it will not be late. During this delay will be the time when faith is challenged, tried, and purified. Noah preached for 120 years while building the Ark, and outside of his own family, had not a single convert. But that was not the real test of his faith. When the Ark was completed and God had drawn all the animals aboard, He spoke to Noah and told him to take his family and come aboard. When Noah and his wife, his three sons, and their wives were aboard, God shut the door.

Then they sat there while nothing happened for seven days (Gen. 7:10).

Can you not picture this scene? Mrs. Noah awakes the first morning and looks outside to a beautiful sunshiny morning. She looks at Noah but says nothing. The second day, the same thing. On the third day, she says, "Noah, it isn't raining yet. Are you sure about all this? I feel like a fool sitting here like a rabbit in a cage." The boys and their wives can be heard off to one side of the room. Mrs. Japheth says, "I think the old man has gone off his rocker." "Shhh," says Shem, "he will hear you." "I don't give a hoot if he does," Mrs. Ham lashes out, "I'm sick and tired of this whole thing. Just get that door open and I am going to get out of here."

While this is happening inside, there is a drunken, jeering, mocking crowd outside. They thump on the hull of the ark and laugh. "Hey Noah, where is the rain? How is the weather in there, Noah? It's fine out here!" And that goes on until the seventh day. But when the seven days were fulfilled, the fountains of the deep burst forth and the heavens opened with a mighty deluge. *You have need of endurance, so that when you have done the will of God, you may receive the promise*" (Heb. 10:36).

Who Can Believe?

We see that men cannot believe God at will, that faith is a gift of God, and that faith comes. But we cannot absolve man of his responsibility to believe. Although he cannot produce faith himself, there are some things which he can do and most certainly ought. Because some will not do these things, and because they do other things that harden their obstinacy and rebellion against God, for these people faith is not possible. It is no good to admonish them to believe. They cannot.

Jesus lists ten reasons why some men cannot believe in John 5:37-44. We read first the rhetorical questions of John 5:44: *"How can you believe?"* The obvious answer is that they cannot. Why can they not?

1. *You have not heard His voice* (John 5:37). Since faith is based upon the Word of God, men who have not heard cannot believe.

2. *You have not seen his shape* (John 5:37). The only eyes you have and physical ones, being spiritually blind, and you can only believe what you can see, and God is invisible.

3. *His Word is not abiding in you* (John 5:38). His Word alone is truth, and without truth there can be no basis for faith.

4. *You will not believe God's messenger* (John 5:38). You have not heard his voice and you will not listen to one who has.

5. *You **think** you have eternal life* (John 5:39). No one is so impossible to move as the person who thinks he has arrived. You are satisfied in your delusion.

6. *You will not come to Christ* (John 5:40). Only Christ can give you faith and you refuse to come to Him.

7. *You do not have the love of God in you* (John 5:42). Not loving God, you would not obey Him, even if you knew His Word and will.

8. *You will not receive one who comes in the name of the Lord* (John 5:43). You think yourself the final judge and authority of all things and will reject the authority of God in another man.

9. *You will receive a man coming in his own name* (John 5:43). This world is tuned to receive the brash, showy, loudmouth, I-know-everything braggart. It has no respect for the meek, humble man. It is looking for a presumptuous, self-willed, aggressive man blowing his own horn. No wonder it stumbles over Christ.

10. *You receive honor one of another* (John 5:44). You have

everything wrapped up between you. You have entered into a pact with men and their organizations so that you will not possibly need God for anything. You have your insurance paid up, your Social Security, your Medicare, your labor union to fight your battles and get the wages you want, and your club and lodge memberships so that you will receive the favored treatment you want. You keep your nose clean with your denomination. You, like the unjust steward, have indebted men to you so that when you need help, they will have to come to your aid. You do not need God. You have made sure that you will never need Him. But you have also cut yourself off as a candidate for faith. Someday you will need something men cannot give you, and then where will you be? Seek honor that comes from God only.

What kind of man, then, can believe God? How does one become a candidate for faith? We have seen that faith must be based on the revealed Word of God, and that before man can believe, he must hear God speak to him. A man, then, who is a candidate for faith must be one who can discern, hear, and know the will of God. He must be able to distinguish the voice of God from two other voices that will attempt to insinuate themselves as God's voice, the voice of the flesh or self from the voice of the devil. We cannot stop the devil from attempting to deceive us, but we can render void his beachhead, the flesh, by the cross of Christ.

*"Therefore, since Christ has suffered in the flesh, arm yourselves also with the same purpose—because he who has suffered in the flesh has ceased from sin—so as to no longer live the rest of the time in the flesh for the lusts of men, but for the **will of God**"* (1 Pet. 4:1-2). A man who is harassed by his uncrucified flesh is not free to consider the will of God. His longing is to satisfy the demands of his belly, his lusts, his ambitions, his petty peeves, and his delights. You must come to a place where you will be perfectly content with any sort of circumstances that

are ordained by God. You can never know the will of God until you are committed to it, whatever it might be. That will not happen until you arm yourself with a mind to willingly partake in the sufferings of Christ in order that sin and rebellion against the perfect will of God in your life will cease.

There has to be a total presentation, an abandonment of one's complete person into the hands of Christ for His use or disposal, according to His good pleasure. In these areas where a total presentation, an absolute surrender, complete obedience, and subjection in all things are recommended and demanded, we are in no wise suggesting that the sinner can come to Christ while *knowingly* making reservations. Certainly one cannot be justified unless he, according to all he knows and understands about himself and these issues of life, makes a total presentation and abandonment of self to Christ. His heart must, at that point, be set on complete obedience or he will never gain hope in Christ Jesus. But as unknown areas are brought to light, as before unknown commandments are made known to him, as cherished sins are revealed to him, as obedience to a special command when the enemy threatens ruin if he obeys God, when these situations in his life face him, then the believer must choose once again to cast his all upon the faithfulness of God.

"Therefore I exhort you, brothers, by the mercies of God, to present your bodies as a sacrifice—living, holy, and pleasing to God, which is your spiritual service of worship. And do not be conformed to this world, but be transformed by the renewing of your mind, so that you may approve what the will of God is, that which is good and pleasing and perfect" (Rom. 12:1-2). We are never told to find the will of God or to get in the will of God. That is something we cannot do.

If God should choose to hide His will from us, we surely could not find it. If He desires to reveal His will to us, then we cannot keep from knowing it. We are simply told to present our bodies and abandon them at His feet alive for His use. As we do this, He accepts us and begins to transform our minds. He puts us in His will, and as we begin to know Him, we can see it proved that the guidance that we have received has really been His perfect will. Our responsibility is the presentation. His is the revelation.

Discerning the Voice of the Lord

We are often asked, "How can I tell whether it is God speaking to me or the devil?" Now anyone who tells you it is easy is a novice. It is not easy because the enemy is subtle, and he knows us well. He is a master at deceit. There are no few quick tricks you can learn which will assure you that you will never be deceived. There are, however, some unvarying principles which you must learn and then you simply have to learn by experience to know the voice of the Master.

All Christians have discernment by nature of the life of Christ that is within them, yet discernment is a sense that must be exercised and developed through use. *"But solid food is for the mature, who because of **practice** have their **senses trained to discern both good and evil**"* (Heb. 5:14). As you begin to exercise these senses of discernment, you will make some mistakes, but every single mistake teaches you something about the Lord and about the enemy. Jesus said, *"**Learn from Me, for I am gentle and humble in heart, and you will find rest for your souls**"* (Matt. 11:29). There is no way to achieve instant maturity. You grow and learn to know the Lord. But here are some guiding principles.

1. The cross of Christ must have rendered you neutral so far as self-will is concerned. *"He who has suffered in the flesh has ceased from sin— so as to no longer live the rest of the time in the flesh for the lusts of men, but for the will of God"* (1 Pet. 4:1-

2). Three times Christ prayed in the garden, *"Not My will, but Yours be done"* (Matt. 26:36-46). You must truly rid yourself of all your personal goals. Especially treacherous are these high-sounding religious objectives and longings: a great ministry, power to witness, a special gift, and so forth. You must have truly presented yourself for Christ and His use according to Romans 12:1. It is only then that you can be pleased with what God says, no matter what it is.

2. Know the truth. Get a good working knowledge of the Bible. The Holy Spirit does not cross Himself by saying one thing in the Bible and then leading you to do something contrary to Scriptural principles.

3. *"Commit your works to Yahweh and your plans will be established"* (Prov. 16:3). Proceed in a normal course of life, trusting the Lord to establish and order your thoughts as he has promised to do for those whose only desire is to work the works of God. Trust Him to check you in spirit or in providence if you are about to take the wrong step. Listen for His voice. He is able to guide you. Give Him credit for doing what He has promised to do. You do not have to strain and fret over every little decision. He is more able to speak and cause you to hear than you realize.

4. In matters of great importance where there is no definitely revealed word, do not move until you are constrained to move. If there is uneasiness about the move, wait for a more sure word. God can make you certain. You can afford to wait until you are. You are not going to miss anything by waiting, and God is not going to scold or punish you while you are testing the spirits. Did He not command you to do so (1 John 4:1)? Consider His patience with Gideon.

5. The Holy Spirit is consistent and persistent. God is immutable. He does not change. If, while waiting, you have a number of different impressions, each one seeming better than the previous one, throw them all out. The Holy Spirit

leads you in only one direction. He will never change His Mind about that. The same leadership will continue to persist until you obey.

6. The Holy Spirit does not drive and demand. It is the devil who puts you in a rush and demands that you act immediately. You will feel that if you take time to pray and wait, you will miss something. Do not listen to that spirit. It is not God but the devil. God will lead you and give you time to consider until you are fully persuaded. And there will be peace in the action, not pressure and torment.

7. Look for providence. God sponsors what He initiates. He provides the way and clears the obstacles. He opens the appropriate doors. The devil can cause hindrances, but he cannot stop what God has led you to do. As you proceed, God will confirm you, or He will stop you.

When Faith Becomes Possible

Faith becomes possible when God speaks to a man for whom faith is possible. (You read that correctly.) We will elaborate on this a little further along.

Several years ago, I was attending a Bible conference where my good friend, Manley Beasley, was ministering. At the time I was under a tremendous burden. I was at an important crossroads in Christian growth and it seemed that if I were to continue on to follow the Lord it would cost me everything, ruin me that is, unless God marvelously and miraculously intervened.

Brother Beasley made one statement that evening which the Holy Spirit so profoundly impressed upon me that I had to get up and leave the meeting immediately and meditate on what had just been shown to me. This is what he said: "A need is positive evidence of God's abundant supply to meet that need. In fact, the need is created to bring us to the supply." The sheer force of that truth hit me like a sledge-hammer and I had to commit myself to it. When I did, the Lord immediately intervened and supplied my need in a precious and blessed way.

I happily walked in that light for some time before another problem began to materialize. I was having trouble identifying what a legitimate need was. Sometimes I could create my own needs. Sometimes "needs" were only carnal desires, ambitions, or objectives of my own. How was I to identify a legitimate need? I found the answer in the substance of Dietrich Bonhoeffer's *The Cost of Discipleship*. Bonhoeffer ties faith and obedience so closely together that he states the double truth. "Only those who believe can obey, and only those who obey can believe."

As God speaks and we obey, we are thrust into a situation whereby if God is not faithful we are ruined.

Here is Brother Beasley's full statement:

"Faith becomes possible when, in obedience to a call or command of God, a need is created that only God can meet. It is obedience to God that creates a legitimate need. And such needs will certainly, without fail, be met, even if God has to move heaven and hell to do so.

The Christian life, the life of the justified, thus becomes a life of faith. The just shall live by his faith. It is not only a life that is lived with a constant eye upon God, looking to Him continuously, but it is a life that is filled with crises. As we walk in obedience to God, we are repeatedly called upon to face impossible situations. Our obedience in these circumstances will threaten to prove our ruin. But it is in just such a trial that our faith is purified and perfected, and we come to know the Lord in all His power and glory.

The ultimate objective of these trials of faith from God's stand-point is to teach us His faithfulness. He wants us to worship and adore Him and we cannot do it because we do not appreciate Him fully. But every time we, by obedience to His commands, are faced with these desperate needs, we see His abundant supply coming to our rescue just in time. We learn that He can be trusted. We discover that His Word cannot fail. We find that there are no circumstances, no matter how impossible, that He cannot instantly change in order to fulfill His promises. We are thus drawn irresistibly to worship and adore Him. More and more our desires are to cling more closely to Him and to be conformed to the image of His Son. We learn of Him and find rest unto our souls."

Insights from Christendom

"The first act of saving faith consists in a discovery and sight of the infinite greatness, goodness, and other excellencies of the nature of God, so as to judge it our duty upon His call, His command, and promise, to deny ourselves, to relinquish all things, and to do so accordingly.

The formal object of faith in the Divine promises, is not the things promised in the first place, but God Himself in His essential excellencies, of truth, or faithfulness and power.

It is the nature of faith to mortify, not only corrupt and sinful lusts, but our natural affections and their most vehement inclinations, though in themselves innocent, if they are any way uncompliant with duties of obedience to the commands of God... ye herein lies the principle trial of the sincerity and power of faith.

Where faith enables men to live unto God, as unto their eternal concerns, it will enable them to trust unto Him in all the difficulties, dangers, and hazards of this life. To pretend a trust in God as unto our souls and invisible things, and not resign our temporal concerns with patience and quietness unto His disposal, is a vain pretense. Too many deceive themselves with a presumption of faith in the promises of God, as unto things future and eternal. They suppose that they do so believe, as that they shall be eternally saved, but if they are brought into any trial, as unto things temporal, wherein they are concerned, they know not what belongs unto the life of faith, nor how to trust God in a due manner."

JOHN OWEN

*"A promise from God may very instructively be compared to a check payable to order. It is given to the believer with the view of bestowing upon him some good thing. It is not meant that he should read it comfortably, and then have done with it. No, he is to treat the promise as a reality, as a man treats a check. He is to take the promise and endorse it with his own name by personally receiving it as true. **He is by faith to accept it as his own.** He sets his seal that God is true, and true to this particular word of promise. He goes further, and believes that he has the blessing in having the sure promise of it, and therefore he puts his name to it to testify to the receipt of the blessing. This done, he must believingly present the promise to the Lord, as a man presents a check at the counter of a bank. He must plead it by prayer, expecting to have it fulfilled. If he has come to Heaven's bank at the right date, he will receive the promised amount at once. If the date should happen to be further on, he must patiently wait till its arrival; but meanwhile he may count the promise as money, for the bank is sure to pay when the due time arrives. Some fail to place the endorsement of faith upon the check, and so they get nothing; others are slack in presenting it, and these also receive nothing. This is not the fault of the promise, but of those who do not act with it in a common-sense, business like manner. God has given no pledge which He will not redeem, and encouraged no hope which He will not fulfill."*

CHARLES SPURGEON

Meditating on the Word

Read and reflect on Hebrews 10:35-11:2, Hebrews 11:11, Habakkuk 2:1-4, and John 5:37-44.

Read James 1:5-8 and Ephesians 5:15-16. Remember when in need of wisdom or discernment we can ask the Lord because He cares for us.

Read Matthew 6:25-34. Remember, if God has not

forbidden something in His Word and we have a personal desire for it, we should not worry. Instead we should trust in His promise in Psalm 37:4. This verse suggests that when we delight in Him, our desires become aligned with His will, indicating they are not necessarily sinful or outside of His will. Seek His Word, continue in prayer, and test the spirits. The Lord will direct your path (Prov. 3:5-8).

Questions for Reflection

1. What is the ultimate goal of faith?
2. What is the dominating act of faith from man's side?
3. Can you list four ways that faith does not come?
4. How does faith actually come?
5. What insights about faith can we gain from Habakkuk 2:1-4?
6. What are the five key elements of genuine faith?
7. According to Jesus in John 5:37-44, what are ten reasons why some people cannot believe?
8. What are the seven guiding principles for discerning the voice of the Lord?
9. According to Dietrich Bonhoeffer, how is faith made possible?
10. What insights about faith has God revealed to you in this chapter?

For Further Reading

Read *All of Grace* by Charles Spurgeon.

6

———

GREAT FAITH

WE HAVE SAID that faith is the most important subject in the Bible. In this closing chapter, we will demonstrate great faith by trying faith with another primary Bible principle, which is authority.

All of the foundational principles of the Bible are found in the book of Genesis, so we want to take our first reference from Genesis 2:16: *"And Yahweh God commanded the man, saying..."* Significantly, this is the first record of communication between man and God after man had been created. It lays the foundation which will establish the proper relationship between God and man so long as man inhabits His creation. It will ensure the welfare, safety, and happiness of man. It will render the proper honor and glory accorded to God. The principle is very simple: God commands man with absolute and unquestioned authority, while the required total submission of man is to the law of God.

Absolute Authority

We must not think that law ended with the Old Testament no more than we should think grace began with the New Testament. Noah found grace in the eyes of God, and such grace as Noah found is no different than the grace and truth that came by Christ Jesus. The teachings of Jesus in the Sermon on the Mount are no less law than that which Moses brought down from Sinai. Man is never without law to God and never will be. It is the only reasonable relationship between creature and Creator.

Enlightened men know that the absolute and unchanging law of God, His sovereign rule over their lives, is for their benefit. It is an unspeakable comfort, a delight and joy. They have been taught by the Spirit as to the sweet security of unquestioned obedience to His wise and gracious counsel. Before Satan rebelled, there was only one will in the universe: the will of God. After Satan rebelled, there were two wills in the universe: the will of God and the will of Satan. When man was introduced into the universe with free will, God made provision to protect him from falling into the will of the devil. Man was to be obedient to the will of God. As long as he was so obedient, he would never do the will of Satan and so fall under his power.

God ordained everything in the beginning with absolute law. It was never to change, and God has not changed His mind about that. Indeed He has ordained a time when every-thing will once again be put under His feet.

As we now examine the apostle Paul's second letter to the Thessalonians, we will see the way things are working in this present evil age.

"For the mystery of lawlessness is already at work; only he who now restrains will do so until he is taken out of the way. And then

that lawless one will be revealed—whom the Lord Jesus will slay with the breath of His mouth and bring to an end by the appearance of His coming—whose coming is in accord with the working of Satan, with all power and signs and false wonders, and with all the deception of unrighteousness for those who perish, because they did not receive the love of the truth so as to be saved. And for this reason God sends upon them a deluding influence so that they will believe what is false, in order that they all may be judged who did not believe the truth, but took pleasure in unrighteousness" (2 Thessalonians 2:7-12).

The word that arrests our attention here is in 2 Thessalonians 2:7. Lawlessness, translated from the Greek *anomia*, is the mystery that is working out through the course of the age. The perfect order of God is seen in absolute law. The fallen aversion from man toward the rule of God is seen more and more through the course of the age until the age closes in the full revelation of the utter lawlessness of ruined men.

We receive a look at this revealed lawlessness in the little book of Jude, which has sometimes been called "The Acts of the Apostates." It is a fitting title. It is also not without significance that the New Testament church age opens with the Acts of the Apostles and closes with the Acts of the Apostates. The Acts of the Apostles is a record and testimony of the character and deeds of those who believe and obey God. The Acts of the Apostates is a record and testimony of the character and deeds of those who disbelieve and disobey God. As faith, obedience, and salvation are inseparable, so unbelief, disobedience, and apostasy are inseparable.

Without venturing too far into the book of Jude, we can examine a few verses and see the characteristics of apostates. *"Yet in the same way these men, also by dreaming"* (Jude 8). They are dreamers. They will not face reality. They have refused all objective truth and made everything subject to what they are experiencing or what they think they are experiencing. The direct light of truth to them is too harsh for their eyes accustomed to darkness. They want to fantasize, and when they are presented with any information, they want that information in an oblique way.

Is it not significant that the most popular means of "presenting the Gospel" today is through puppet shows, ventriloquist acts in which you have another dummy beside the preacher, magic shows, and religious movies? Now people know very well the performers in the movie are only pretending to pray or preach or repent, and they know quite well that magic is a trick and that dummies do not speak. But they like to dream! Why? They are filthy! They cannot bear the unmitigated truth of the Word of God.

They would rather pretend that the Word is a game so that they can continue in their wicked rebellion. They tell themselves that if the means is a fake, then so is the message. The sword has no edge and the hammer has no force. It degenerates into third-rate religious entertainment for people who would be happier with less mind than they have.

"Defile the flesh" (Jude 8). They prostitute their bodies for their own base pleasures. I am not speaking of the street-walkers in the red-light districts who sell their bodies. I am speaking of those ordinary people who every day, defile, indulge, abuse, ruin, and corrupt their own bodies in an ever-increasing attempt to satiate their insatiable lusts.

"Reject authority" (Jude 8). They hate anything that stands for rule, order, dominion, or authority. They will not be restrained from that which they wish to do. No more does an ordinance appear than they hate that ordinance; no more do they hear of a law than they lust to break that law. No more does a precept appear than they trample that precept.

"Blaspheme glorious ones" (Jude 8). They rail against

authorities. They curse their magistrates, lambast their governors and presidents, and revile their employers and supervisors. Are you not familiar with this, dear friend?

"They have gone the way of Cain" (Jude 11). The way of Cain is the way of a man who does that which is right in his own eyes. He ignored the Word of God, worshiped to please himself, and brought to God the fruit of the ground that He had cursed. Refusing the sin offering, he rose up against his righteous brother and murdered him, lied to God, refused to confess his sin, died, and went to hell.

"They have poured themselves into the error of Balaam" (Jude 11). Balaam is the covetous hireling. Unable to curse the people of God, he found a way to earn money from Balak by advising him to seduce the people of God into adultery and idolatry. It is still the way of hireling preachers. Is it not true that many so-called preachers are paid solely because they *will not* preach the truth? If they did preach the truth, they would no longer be paid.

"Perished in the rebellion of Korah" (Jude 11). In Numbers 16, Korah decided that Moses the man of God had too much authority and gathered 250 big-shot Israelites with the objective of taking the preacher down a peg or two. Korah is the pioneer of the "Lay Movement." *"You have gone far enough, for all the congregation are holy, every one of them, and Yahweh is in their midst"* (Num. 16:3). God showed in no uncertain terms His disapproval of such rebellion. He did an entirely new thing for them: opened the earth beneath them and sent them all to hell alive! You want to be very sure you do not become a part of the rebellious posterity of Korah.

The Laws of Authority

Having now seen the foundational nature of authority and the tendency of man to throw off authority during the

course of the age, and the ultimate rebellion that characterizes the end time, we will now consider the laws embodied in
the principle of authority.

*"Every person is to be in subjection to the governing authorities.
For there is no authority except from God, and those which exist
have been appointed by God. Therefore whoever resists that
authority has opposed the ordinance of God; and they who have
opposed will receive condemnation upon themselves. For rulers are
not a cause of fear for good behavior, but for evil. Do you want to
have no fear of that authority? Do what is good, and you will have
praise from the same; for it is a minister of God to you for good.
But if you do what is evil, be afraid; for it does not bear the sword
in vain, for it is a minister of God, an avenger who brings wrath on
the one who practices evil"* (Romans 13:1-4).

From these verses, we can glean a number of facts and
unchangeable laws concerning authority. The word *exousia*
in Greek translates as "power" sixty-nine times, "authority"
twenty-nine times, "right" twice, "liberty" once, "jurisdiction"
once, and "strength" once within the New Testament. Let us
now look at the word *authority* as it relates to this passage.

1. *Every soul **has** a higher authority.* It is not said that every
soul ought to have a higher authority but it is expressly
declared that he has one by the admonition that he is subject
to it. Simply put, everyone has a boss. This applies not only
to the realm of men but to the animal world. If it is nothing
but a herd of cattle in a pasture, there is either a bull or a
boss cow in that pasture, and they all are aware of the butting
order. If it is nothing but ants in an anthill, there is a boss ant
there, with a chain of command through the lesser ants that
keep the whole complex made up of thousands of ants in
perfect order.

I was staying in a home some years ago where one of the

teenage girls had a birthday. She was involved in 4-H work and was given some bantam chickens by various people. They had to prepare a pen for them. When the little pen was finished and the chickens deposited, one of the children came running in and crying, "They are fighting, the chickens are fighting each other." "Just let them alone," I said. "They will settle down as soon as they get the pecking order straightened out." Sure enough, in a little while, the head chicken was established and they all were walking around singing contentedly. Would that men could settle things so quickly!

2. *That authority is ordained by God.* Regardless of the circumstances of the placing of any given authority, God saw to it that he was placed in the position that he is in. Whether by political process, birth, marriage, employment, or choice, throughout the whole ordeal God saw to it that the authority was installed. You cannot believe Romans 8:28, Ephesians 1:11, or Daniel 4:25 if you do not believe this. If the principle of Genesis 2:16 yet stands, and it does, since the laws of God are immutable, then God surely has ordained authority wherever that authority appears.

3. *All are commanded to be subject to that authority* (see Appendix D). We may not choose whether we will obey this authority on the basis of who the authority is, whether good or bad. We are commanded by God to be obedient to His ordained authority.

4. *That authority is the minister of God to you for good.* Regardless of who he is, he is the minister of God. He may be an infidel, yet he is still a minister of God to you for your good. Wife, your husband is the best man on earth for you. Children, your parents are the best on earth for you. Man, that wicked, miserly, unreasonable employer is the best boss on earth for you. Be careful that you do not contradict your confidence in the Word of God here. Although you may not

be able in your circumstances to see this truth, you must confess and embrace it, since all the precepts of God are good and right.

5. *That authority is a terror to evil.* "Evil" can properly be considered in a personal sense here. The authority of God terrorizes the evil one. He is the protection of God over you against the devil.

6. *To resist that authority is to resist God Himself.* Rebellion against authority ordained by God is tantamount to direct rebellion against God. To spurn the ambassador of the King, His Vicar, is to insult His Majesty Himself. God commands the man. He rules him through His ordained order of authority. Receiving orders from the authority is a reception of orders from God insofar as this principle extends.

7. *All who resist or rebel against the authority voluntarily bring damnation, judgment, and hell upon themselves.* They have deliberately made themselves a bed in hell. They have brought upon themselves more misery, trouble, and bondage than they ever reckoned, and they have no one to blame or thank but themselves and their rebellion.

The Sin of Rebellion

Please now consider the full implications of the sin of rebellion. For an illustration, we will look at a scene in the Old Testament. This is the setting: God has commanded Saul the king of Israel to *"go and strike Amalek and devote to destruction all that he has, and do not spare him; but put to death both man and woman, infant and nursing baby, ox and sheep, camel and donkey"* (1 Sam. 15:3). Saul, however, failed to obey the Lord completely. Foolishly thinking he knew better than God what ought to be done, he spared the Amalekite king, Agag, and the best of the sheep, the oxen, the fatlings, and the lambs (1 Sam. 15:8-9). He only destroyed that which he considered inferior.

Such partial obedience is nothing less than outright disobedience. The man who edits and censors the commands of God, who obeys only that which seems reasonable to him, is no more obedient to God than the confessed unbeliever. He is just as much a rebel as ever. God is not King, he is.

Now the Word of the Lord comes to the prophet Samuel. *"I regret that I have made Saul king, for he has turned back from following Me and has not established My words"* (1 Sam. 15:11). As Samuel ventures out to meet Saul on his return he is greeted with the hypocritical bragging of a self-willed rebel. *"Blessed are you of Yahweh! I have established the word of Yahweh"* (1 Sam. 15:13). But the bleating of sheep and lowing of oxen contradict his boast.

It will be always so with you, dear reader. You may boast convincingly about your faith and submission to God, but the fruits of your rebellion and disobedience will drown out your lies. No one will believe you.

Now see the awful implications of rebellion. *"And Samuel said, 'Has Yahweh as much delight in burnt offerings and sacrifices as in obeying the voice of Yahweh? Behold, to obey is better than sacrifice, and to heed than the fat of rams. For rebellion is as the sin of divination, and insubordination is as wickedness and idolatry. Because you have rejected the word of Yahweh, He has also rejected you from being king'"* (1 Sam. 15:22-23). The words "is as" in 1 Samuel 15:23 are not in the original text, but are inserted to increase the readability of the passage. But the passage has more force if they are left out.

Notice that rebellion, the sin of *divination* or *witchcraft,* and insubordination or stubbornness, *wickedness* and *idolatry.* We saw in the second chapter that unbelief always serves other gods and that to turn from God is to turn to idols.

Now the Bible has plainly made rebellion and witchcraft,

stubbornness and idolatry to be synonymous. How about it, dear reader? Are you a witch? Are you an idolator? Of course not, you say. Yet according to the Word of God, if you are unbelieving and rebellious, you are a witch. If you stubbornly resist the commandments of God, you are an idolator. Demon worship is not something strange and foreign to you because you practice it. Why should you be shocked with reports about Satanic cults? You have had your own for years! Unbelief, rebellion, witchcraft, stubbornness, idolatry, and demon possession are all part of the same package.

Consider the following warning from the New Testament:

"But I want you to understand that Christ is the head of every man, and the man is the head of a woman, and God is the head of Christ. Every man who has something on his head while praying or prophesying, shames his head. But every woman who has her head uncovered while praying or prophesying, shames her head, for she is one and the same as the woman whose head is shaved. For if a woman does not cover her head, let her also have her hair cut short. But if it is disgraceful for a woman to have her hair cut short or her head shaved, let her cover her head. For a man ought not to have his head covered, since he is the image and glory of God, but the woman is the glory of man. For man does not originate from woman, but woman from man. For indeed man was not created for the woman's sake, but woman for the man's sake. Therefore the woman ought to have a symbol of authority on her head, because of the angels" (1 Corinthians 11:3-10).

We are told further in 1 Corinthians 11:14-15 that even nature teaches us that it is a shame for a man to have long hair and that the hair of a woman, being long, is a glory to her, for the hair is given to her for a covering. There is more than a coincidence in the modern trend toward short hair on women and long hair on men, feminine clothes on men and masculine clothes on women. It is all part of the latter-day rebellion. There is a natural difference between male and female, and God has seen to it that this difference is to be noted, observed, and kept.

Nature teaches it. The difference is readily recognized in the animal world. In such beasts as cats, dogs, horses, and cattle, physical configuration reveals the sex. In creatures where this configuration is concealed, God has dressed the male and female in distinctly different garments so that anyone can tell a rooster from a hen.

God has likewise demanded that there be at least two ways to distinguish a man from a woman: the garments they wear and the relative length of their hair. However long a man's hair is, it ought to be shorter than a woman's, and a woman's longer than a man's. Whatever a woman wears, it ought to be distinctly feminine, and the garments of a man must be unmistakably masculine. A little child should be able to look at his parents and tell which one is his father and which is his mother without their undressing. Otherwise he will have trouble identifying with the one he should. For this reason, millions grow up to be lesbians and homosexuals.

But the passage to which we wish to direct our attention now is 1 Corinthians 11:10. The woman should have a symbol of authority on her head because of the angels. The symbol or token of the submission of a woman to her husband was a covering that she wore in public. A woman who wore no such covering indicated that she was not subject to a man. It was especially important, the apostle tells us, that a woman wears this covering and so displays her obedience when she participates in worship because of the angels.

Why angels? We must remember that not all angels are good. A third part of them joined Satan in his rebellion (Rev.

12:4). These seem to be one and the same as the wicked spirits, principalities, and powers that are more commonly known as demons. They are emissaries of Satan and only wait for an opportunity to take advantage of someone unsheltered by God.

Submission to the man's authority is the woman's protection against these fallen angels, just as man's submission to Christ, who is his head, is his protection or covering against demons. God commands, rules, and protects all His creatures in this way. In the family unit, this is illustrated as Christ under God, man under Christ, the woman under man, and the children under the parents. Other social units also have a like order established whereby God rules and protects each. Rebelling against the higher authority which is ordained of God is equivalent to serving notice that one is displeased with the way God is ordering his life and issuing an invitation to the devil to replace God as his King. Satan will surely take you up on that.

Several years ago, when we were experiencing this worldwide outbreak of rebellion, I thought that it was caused by a worldwide invasion of demons. The two are related, but I had the cause and effect reversed. For the past several decades, we have had progressively less doctrinal content in our preaching and teaching. The god of success and growth demands that we ignore the long and tedious process of teaching and preaching sound truth, and instead move on with the business of producing more spurious converts.

As true doctrine faded from the picture, authority had no absolutes upon which to rest. Situational ethics, every man doing that which is right in his own eyes, became the vogue. With this philosophy, human authority anywhere became openly despised. Every law and every magistrate was subject to contempt. Rebellion broke out everywhere: children against parents, wives against husbands, students against teachers, citizens against governments, and labor against management. Satan has so many invitations for demons that hell must have been taxed to supply them. That is why, dear reader, we are today experiencing such a revival in devil worship. Everyone has thrown off their covering and invited hell to come and rule over them.

I quite well know that this is not what men intended. They only wanted their liberty to do as they pleased. But in any case they met the conditions of witchcraft and idolatry, and the occult powers immediately accepted the invitation. Several years ago, I left a city after closing a series of meetings on a Sunday night and headed for my home about 250 miles away. I had reached a stretch of highway about ninety miles long with several small towns ten or fifteen miles apart which had speed limits of 25 miles per hour. I was driving the legal speed limit, which was then 60 miles per hour on the open road, slowing down for each small town. But the time had already entered into the early hours of the morning. I was tired and my mind became dull. Driving in a semi-stupor, suddenly four realities registered in my mind simultaneously: a speed limit sign posting 35 miles per hour, one posting 25 miles per hour, my own speedometer registering 55 miles per hour, and a police car parked by the side of the road at the point I was now passing. I immediately snapped to attention, slowed down gently, and tried to creep on through town while watching the police car in my rearview mirror. But it was too late. Here he came with his blue light flashing.

Now I did not intend for that to happen, but I had broken the established law. I was inside the city limits and I was completely under the power and authority of the city of Oberlin. They could have legally taken my car and locked me up. Just as surely, dear reader, as you break the laws of God and rebel against His authority, you fall under the sphere and authority of the devil, and he will not fail to avail himself of this advantage.

The Heritage of the Obedient

So much for the negative side. Now for the positive benefits of submission to authority, we will consider, for illustration, the encounter of a Roman soldier with Christ.

"And a centurion's slave, who was highly regarded by him, was sick and about to die. Now when he heard about Jesus, he sent some Jewish elders asking Him to come and save the life of his slave. And when they came to Jesus, they were earnestly pleading with Him, saying, 'He is worthy for You to grant this to him; for he loves our nation and it was he who built us our synagogue.' Now Jesus was going on His way with them; and when He was not far from the house, the centurion sent friends, saying to Him, 'Lord, do not trouble Yourself further, for I am not good enough for You to come under my roof. For this reason I did not even consider myself worthy to come to You, but just say the word, and my servant will be healed. For I also am a man placed under authority, with soldiers under me; and I say to this one, "Go!" and he goes, and to another, "Come!" and he comes, and to my slave, "Do this!" and he does it.' Now when Jesus heard this, He marveled at him. And He turned to the crowd that was following Him and said, 'I say to you, not even in Israel have I found such great faith'" (Luke 7:2-9).

Now here is a remarkable statement. Jesus is saying that in this man, He has found a greater faith than He has seen anywhere else in all of His earthly ministry! Does that not stir us? How many of us would like to have the Lord say unto us, "You have such great faith." If we can learn what the centurion knew, perhaps we can also have this great faith.

How is it that this Roman soldier, a stranger from the

commonwealth of Israel who had no access to the great theological teachings of the Scriptures, had faith that shamed the doctors, priests, Pharisees, and Sadducees of the day? The fact of the matter is he probably knew little or nothing of faith. It would not be surprising if he were unable to give a reasonable definition of the word.

He was not a theologian. He was a soldier, but as a soldier, the principle he had learned and understood well fitted him for great faith. That principle was authority. He knew how authority worked. He lived and worked in a realm that demanded absolute obedience to the higher authority and had seen its unfailing principles in operation.

Now you, dear reader, are not likely a theologian either, but you need not be to have great faith. You need not understand all the ramifications of faith, but if you can learn what this centurion knew about authority, and make it a principle and practice in your life as it was in his, then your faith will know no bounds.

You see, my friend, your problem is not primarily a faith problem, but an authority problem. You have a faith problem, true enough, but you are never going to get faith by trying to get faith. You must learn to live within the principle of Genesis 2:16. The Lord God commanded the man.

Notice the boldness of the message from the centurion to the Lord as He neared his home. *"Lord, do not trouble Yourself further, for I am not good enough for You to come under my roof. For this reason I did not even consider myself worthy to come to You, but **just say the word, and my servant will be healed**."* He was not trying to assert his faith or advance his opinion by prefacing what he said with "I believe" this or that. He was not speaking from theory or conviction. He was speaking from what he *knew to be true*. He makes no allowances for it to be otherwise. He *knows* that if Christ speaks, the spoken Word has assured the finished work.

How does he know that? We are told precisely how he knows. *"For I **also** am a man placed **under** authority, with soldiers **under** me."* The two key words to be noted here are *also* and *under*: the first because he recognized that Christ was *also* as much subject to a higher authority as he was, and the second because the key to having authority is not getting over someone, but by getting *under* someone. Being under, he is over. You cannot *get* over; you can only *get* under. But if you are under, then you are over all that he whom you are under has placed you over in the same capacity he is over. Think awhile on that. Get hold of that principle and you will never be the same.

The centurion knows it works. When he wants something done, he does not have to move anywhere. He does not have to throw his weight around or spend a lot of energy and words begging, threatening, enticing, persuading, or cajoling. All he does is tell someone to do it and that someone does it. *"I say to this one, 'Go!' and he goes, and to another, 'Come!' and he comes, and to my slave, 'Do this!' and he does it."*

Now why do these hardened soldiers obey this centurion so readily? Is it because they fear him? Has he gained his position of authority by whipping every man in his charge with his bare fists? Does he carry a better sword than they? Is he so much bigger and stronger that they fear him? None of these. The centurion may well have been a small 140-pound weakling and the soldier who obeyed him so readily may have been a 250-pound brute. That soldier was not subjected to the intrinsic authority of the centurion. He was not afraid of him. He was afraid of the Roman Empire. The legions of Caesar stood behind every word that centurion spoke, as long as he was *under* his superior authority.

But now suppose one day the centurion received some orders of which he so disapproved that he disobeyed them and went to do whatever he thought best. What would be the immediate result of such rebellion? His rank would be stripped away and he would be relieved of his command. What then would be his standing with that 250-pound soldier he had so easily subjugated? In all likelihood, he would fear for his bodily safety. He would try to stay out of his way and hope their paths did not cross. When one gets out from authority, he not only loses all of his authority, but also all of his protection. If you are not under, then you *are* under all that you would be over if you were under. Whereas all of the demons of Satan are under your feet as you are submitted to Christ, rebel against Him and you are nothing but meat for the serpents. In other words, you are dust (Gen. 3:14). You are prey to the powers of darkness and victim of all that man would desire to do with you.

There is no authority but from God (Rom. 13:1). Wherever authority exists is from God. If you would gain authority, it must be bestowed upon you by God, and God bestows authority upon those who submit themselves to His authority.

Pastor, would you gain authority over your flock? You will never gain it by trying to assert it. Get under obedience and absolute subjection to Jesus Christ, and His authority will rest upon you. The flock of God will know it and will without fail submit themselves to your leadership. But you can never have authority in disobedience to God.

Husband, would you gain the submission of your wife? Would you rule your house well, as the Scriptures say you must? You cannot make your wife obedient by trying to overcome her rebellion. You will never, either by clever words and subtle devices, or by loud threats and physical abuse, rule that woman. If you would have authority over your home, submit to Christ. If you have no authority, you may be sure you are not properly submitted to the Lord. When you submit to Christ in all things, your wife *will* most assuredly submit to you. She must because the authority of God upon you will demand it.

Wives, do you wonder why your children are disobedient and disrespectful toward you? Do you despair of their rebellion? Wonder no longer. You are disobedient and disrespectful of your husband. The only authority you can possibly have over your children is that which comes from God. You cannot get it from God; you must get it from your husband. That is how He bestows it. Submit yourself to your husband, and the spirit of rebellion will flee your children.

I know some of my readers are going to have difficulty believing the above facts. But are we not yet talking about faith? How did the centurion come to say, *"Just say the word, and my servant will be healed"*? Was it not a confidence that came by *practicing* and *doing* what authority promises? Was it not in this that he learned that when authority speaks, the work will be done? Yes, and he learned it in the realm of human government. If his word spoken under the authority of Caesar could not fail, then how could the Word of Christ, who was under the authority of God?

Even so, dear friend, you must learn that as you submit and obey the Word that God has spoken, the words that you speak *in obedience* to that Word will surely come to pass. The authority of the Eternal God is upon you to see that nothing shall fail. *"If God is for us, who is against us?"* (Rom. 8:31). Doubtless many shall be against us, but none can prevail against us. Shall He who spared not His own Son be frustrated in His purpose to give us all things? It is God that has justified, and God that has promised. He cannot fail.

Learn to appropriate as Joshua did. The principle still stands. Here is the promise: *"No man will be able to stand before you all the days of your life. Just as I have been with Moses, I will be with you; I will not fail you or forsake you"* (Josh. 1:5). What are the conditions? There is merely one. *"Only be strong and very courageous to be careful to* **do according to all the law which Moses My servant commanded you; do not turn aside from it to the right or to the left, so that you may be prosperous wherever you go**" (Josh. 1:7).

At any time Joshua may have had occasion to doubt, he needed only to remember the Word of God, *"Have I not commanded you?"* (Josh. 1:9). Knowing that God had commanded and sent him in obedience to that commission, it was impossible for him to fail. No wonder he was such a mighty man of faith. He learned the principles of authority and obedience. When the time came that he needed more daylight to do his job than the course of the sun could afford him, he suspended the natural laws of the celestial bodies by the spoken word of authority. The authority of God is obeyed even by the inanimate creation of the universe. That is the faith that moves mountains and stills the tempest.

The word of faith is ever a word of action. Faith is something you do in view of who God is and in response to what He has said. Believing can never be separated from doing.

In closing, consider the Old Testament foundation for Romans 10:8: *"But what does it say? 'The word is near you, in your mouth and in your heart'—that is, the word of faith which we are preaching."*

*"For this commandment which I am commanding you today is not too difficult for you, nor is it far from you. It is not in heaven, that you should say, 'Who will go up to heaven for us and get it for us and make us hear it, that we may **do it**?' Nor is it beyond the sea, that you should say, 'Who will cross the sea for us and get it for us and make us hear it, that we may **do it**?' But the word is very near you, in your mouth and in your heart, that you may **do it***" (Deuteronomy 30:11-14).

Three times *"do it"* appears. There it is, dear reader.

God has shown you what you should do. Do it. Are you fearful? Do it! Do you doubt? Do it! You will never know faith or God until you do. Do it!

"Therefore, laying aside all filthiness and all that remains of wickedness, in gentleness receive the implanted word, which is able to save your souls. But become doers of the word, and not merely hearers who delude themselves. For if anyone is a hearer of the word and not a doer, he is like a man who looks at his natural face in a mirror; for once he looked at himself and has gone away, he immediately forgot what kind of person he was. But one who looks intently at the perfect law, the law of freedom, and abides by it, not having become a forgetful hearer but a doer of the work, this man will be blessed in what he does" (James 1:21-25).

Insights from Christendom

"A key verse indicating the importance of the act of believing is John 3:18: 'Whosoever believes in him is not condemned, but whoever does not believe stands condemned already because he has not believed in the name of God's one and only Son.' **The word 'believe' means more than mere credence, a mental acceptance of facts. The root meaning of the word is a personal trust in a person. Such faith causes one to entrust himself completely into the keeping of Jesus Christ, and that surrender will lead him to obey His commands.** *Faith sets a man apart unto God through Jesus Christ for service and worship. By his repentance and faith, he becomes consecrated for holiness. At the moment of conversion, God sanctifies the believing one. Though you were known before*

you were born, a time had to come when you believed in order to receive the salvation the Lord had purchased for you."

JERRY WHITE

Meditating on the Word

Read and reflect on Luke 7:2-9 and John 14:1.

Questions for Reflection

1. What are seven things we know about authority concerning Romans 13:1-4?
2. Outline the six characteristics of apostates.
3. Describe the consequences of disobedience in your own words.
4. Explain the benefits of obedience in your own words.
5. How does understanding authority reinforce our faith?
6. What insights about faith has God revealed to you through this chapter?

For Further Reading

Read *From Death to Life* and *Change of Heart* by Allen S. Nelson IV.

APPENDIX A
A PERSONAL WALK OF FAITH

Insights from Christendom

> *"In the simplest manner in which I am able to express it, I answer:* **Faith is the assurance that the thing which God has said in His Word is true, and that God will act according to what He has said in His Word.** *This assurance, this reliance on God's Word, this confidence is faith."*

GEORGE MULLER

Meditating on the Word

Read and reflect on Hebrews 10:32-12:2, James 2:8, James 2:18, James 2:26, John 1:16, Romans 1:17, and 2 Corinthians 3:18.

Extended Questions for Reflection

1. How should a righteous person live?
2. According to Hebrews 10:39, what do the righteous possess?
3. Identify four aspects of faith revealed in Hebrews 11:1-3.
4. What did Abel and Enoch both do?
5. According to Hebrews 11:4-6, how does a man please God?
6. What insight about faith is revealed in Hebrews 11:7?
7. What does Hebrews 11:8-30 tell us about the faith of the patriarchs?
8. Why is God not ashamed to be called the God of those mentioned in Hebrews 11:16?
9. How did Rahab demonstrate faith in Hebrews 11:31?
10. What does Hebrews 11:32-38 teach us about faith?
11. What is revealed about the object of saving faith in Hebrews 11:39-12:2, Romans 4:1-5, and John 3:14-18?
12. Based on your observations from Hebrews 11:4-40, list at least three consistent outcomes of Biblical faith.
13. How is faith personal?
14. Is there a difference between believing in God and having a personal relationship with Him? If so, what distinguishes the two?
15. Where does your faith currently stand?
16. Remember that experience is not a one-time event but rather a journey of experience throughout your entire life. Where did your personal

experience with faith begin and where has it taken you?

17. Summarize your journey of faith and the lessons that journey has taught you about yourself, humanity, and God.

For Further Reading

Read *Salvation... When?* by Conrad Murrell.

APPENDIX B
AFTER OBEDIENCE, WHAT?

Insights from Christendom

"And immediately Jesus made His disciples get into the boat and go ahead of Him to the other side to Bethsaida, while He Himself was sending the crowd away" (Mark 6:45).

> *"We are apt to imagine that as Jesus Christ constrains us, and we obey Him, He will lead us to great success. We must never put our dreams of success as God's purpose for us; His purpose may be exactly the opposite. We have an idea that God is leading us to a particular end, a desired goal; He is not. The question of getting to a particular end is mere incident.* **What we call the process God calls the end.** *(John 14:15)*
>
> *What is my dream of God's purpose?* **His purpose is that I depend on Him and on His power now.** *If I can stay in the middle of the turmoil calm and perplexed, that is the end of the purpose of God.* **God is not working to a particular finish; His end is the process**—*that I see Him*

walking on the waves, no shore in sight, no success, no goal, just the absolute certainty that it is alright because I see Him walking on the sea. It is the process, not the end, which is glorifying to God.

God's training is for now, not presently. His purpose is for this minute, not for something in the future. We have nothing to do with the afterwards of obedience; we go wrong when we think of the afterward. **What we call training and preparation, God calls the end.** *God's end is to enable me to see that He can walk on the chaos of my life in the here and now. If we have further end in view, we do not pay sufficient attention to the immediate present: If we realize that obedience is the end, then each moment as it comes is precious."*

OSWALD CHAMBERS

APPENDIX C
FAITH MAY BE INCREASED

"Now these were more noble-minded than those in Thessalonica, for they received the word with great eagerness, examining the Scriptures daily to see whether these things were so" (Acts 17:11).

*"**No impressions are to be taken in connection with faith.** Impressions have neither one thing nor the other to do with faith. Faith has to do with the Word of God. It is not impressions strong or weak, which will make any difference. We have to do with the written word not ourselves or our impressions.*

***Neither are probabilities to be taken into account.** Many people are willing to believe regarding those things that seem probable to them. Faith has nothing to do with probabilities. The province of faith begins where probabilities cease and sight and sense fail. A great many of God's children are cast down and lament their want of faith. They write to me and say that they have no impressions, no feel-*

ing, and they see no probability that the thing they wish will come to pass. Appearances are not to be taken into account. **The question is whether or not God has spoken it in His Word.**

'Consider it all joy, my brothers, when you encounter various trials, knowing that the testing of your faith brings about perseverance. And let perseverance have its perfect work, so that you may be perfect and complete, lacking in nothing' (James 1:2-4).

And now, my beloved friends, you are in great need to ask yourselves whether your are in the habit of thus confiding, in your inmost soul, in what God has said, and whether you are in earnest in seeking to find whether the thing you want is in accordance with what He has said in His Word.

You see, God delights to increase the faith of His children. Our faith, which is feeble at first, is developed and strengthened more and more by use. We ought instead of wanting no trials before victory, no exercise for patience, to be willing to take them from God's hand as a means. I say— and say it deliberately—trials, obstacles, difficulties, and sometimes defeats, are the very food of faith. I get letters from so many of God's dear children who say: 'Dear Brother Mueller, I am writing this because I am so weak and feeble in faith.'

Just so surely as we ask to have our faith strengthened, we must feel a willingness to take from God's hand the means for strengthening it. We must allow Him to educate us through trials and bereavements and troubles. It is through trials that faith is exercised and developed more and more. God affectionately permits difficulties that he may develop unceasingly that which He is willing to do for us, and to this end we should not shrink, but if He gives us *sorrow and hindrances and losses and afflictions, we should take them out of His hands as evidences of His love and care for us in developing more and more that faith which He is seeking to strengthen in us."*

GEORGE MULLER

When the doctrine of unquestioned submission to human authority is advanced, the question of conflict with the commandments of God is always brought forth. These questions usually come from those who are not truly interested in how far they must go in obedience, but rather if they can get out of obedience altogether. Often some hypothetical situation is generally advanced, such as "What if the husband demands his wife do such and such a thing?"

Hypothetical suppositions are just that. They cannot be answered because they are not real. Answers exist only for real situations. Many people imagine they know such a real situation, but there are always factors one does not know, and therefore he does not know the whole reality of the thing. Such fears and objections are fabrications of the devil. No one ever takes a step in faith without his threats of "what if" or "suppose such and such." It is enough to say that the woman who obeys her husband needs not have confidence in him. Her confidence is in the God to whose law she has submitted.

God is bigger than the meanness of her husband. Can you

not believe God to protect a woman who so trusts Him? We have at least one Scriptural example to illustrate that He does. *"For in this way in former times the holy women also, who hoped in God, used to adorn themselves, being subject to their own husbands, just as Sarah obeyed Abraham, calling him lord. You have become her children if you do good, not fearing any intimidation"* (1 Pet. 3:5-6). Such obedience twice sent Sarah to the harem of a heathen king from which God faithfully delivered her without a man touching her (Gen. 12:11-20, Gen. 20:2-14). Much destruction has been done to homes by teaching women to rebel against their husbands in order to perform religious duties.

There are limitations, however, to *obedience*, but not to submission. When Shadrach, Meshach, and Abednego refused to worship the image made by the king, they did not do so out of rebellion against the king. They could not transgress the commandment of God for worship, but they did not rebel against the authority of the king. They had an alternative: the burning furnace. They simply chose the only alternative the king gave them. This is a far cry from so-called civil disobedience, which is nothing less than lawlessness that characterizes rebels against what they consider unjust laws. In extreme cases, you may not be able to obey, yet you can submit and trust God to take care of you in the consequences.

ABOUT THE AUTHOR

Conrad Murrell served in evangelistic ministry for over 50 years and was powerfully used by God in many Assemblies of God and Baptist churches in the United States and around the world. Throughout that time, Conrad pastored churches in Texas and Louisiana, successfully hosted numerous Bible conferences, engaged in continuous itinerant preaching, and diligently evangelized throughout the United States and Mexico. In addition to his fruitful ministry, he also wrote several books, many of which are read worldwide today. Mack Tomlinson's biography of Conrad Murrell is a testimony of God's grace and truth in the life of a man called by God for the proclamation of the Gospel.

Conrad Murrell was a significant contemporary and friend to two of the 20th century's leading experts on revival, Leonard Ravenhill and Richard Owen Roberts. He was also a dearly loved co-laborer and associate of several other prominent evangelists of our age, such as Manley Beasley and Al Whittinghill. He was a committed, passionate, and anointed itinerant minister like them. He was a man's man, a man of conviction and grit, but most importantly, he was God's man—a man completely devoted to his Lord and Savior.

To order Conrad Murrell's biography or for more information on the original material concerning his works, please call or email Mack Tomlinson at (940)435-1689 or macknlinda@aol.com.

ABOUT THE PUBLISHER

Grace and Truth Press L.L.C. was founded in 2023 by Mark and Amber Goodson with the aim of creating resources for the church and forging partnerships with like-minded churches,  ministries, and businesses. Our overarching goal is to embody the principles of "All of Christ for All of Life" and "May His Kingdom Ever Increase On Earth As It Is In Heaven" in every aspect of our operations. We strive for nothing less than this comprehensive commitment to Christ. Below are a few of the books we plan to release in 2025.

Visit GraceandTruthPress.com to order now!

BONAFICE
MEDIA

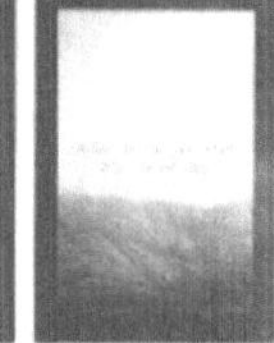

APOLOGETIC

EQUIPPING
MEN

THE
GOSPEL
FORUM

THIRSTING FOR GOD

Sick of woke entertainment?

Try Bonafice Media
for FREE

at BONAFICE.COM